Immerse: A 52-Week Course in Resilient Living

Immerse: A 52-Week Course in Resilient Living

A Commitment to Live With Intentionality,
Deeper Presence, Contentment, and Kindness.

Dr. Amit Sood HD, MD
Professor of Medicine

To all of you who care about building a kinder, happier, and more hopeful world for our planet's children.

To my parents, Sahib and Shashi Sood – my role models of resilience.

Contents

Why Immerse?

I have struggled all my life with self doubt and negative emotions. Some of this struggle, I believe, comes from early childhood experiences. Let me share with you three early strikes I endured as a child that stifled my happiness. First, I must have been six or seven when a bully told me that I didn't belong to my family and that I had been picked up from a garbage dump. I believed his every single word and spent countless hours silently worrying that I would soon be disowned and sent back to where I belonged.

Second, one of our middle-school teachers, in an effort to tame us, cautioned us to stop laughing for frivolous reasons. Expounding his twisted logic, he said something like, "Kids, the numbers of times you laugh and cry are the same in this life. So don't laugh without a good reason, because then you'll have to cry for a good reason." From that day on, I stopped finding it funny when a crow jumped on the back of a donkey or a goat chased a cow. Even if I found something funny, I chose to contain my mirth, worried my giggles might seed a future pain.

Third, as a teenager I witnessed one of the worst industrial disasters of all times; it happened a few miles away from my home. Thousands of people perished in my hometown of Bhopal that night, suffocated by a toxic chemical spill. I remember waking up to the pounding on the door at 2:00 a.m., and then rushing with a sea of humanity, fleeing the fumes of methyl isocyanate.

Two days later, when I showed up at the hospital to help, I was completely unprepared for the suffering I saw. By the time I turned eighteen, I had seen more adversity and misery than most people see in their lifetime.

A decade later, with an MD behind my name and my neural pathways fully myelinated, I wondered about my melancholy. Why did I listen to the bullies and the teacher who didn't care about my wellbeing and not to the many others who loved me? Why did I struggle with accepting the reflection that I saw in the mirror? Why didn't I recognize the examples of real courage and resilience through the tremendous adversity I witnessed? These questions assumed a sense of urgency when I traveled overseas and saw the same stress and suffering, without the scourge of chemical spill or abject poverty to explain them. Lucky for me, I was asking these questions when thousands of evolutionary biologists, neuroscientists, psychologists, and philosophers had already begun to piece the answers together.

Talking to them, and learning from their writings, I realized that a confluence of three powerful forces seed unhappiness.

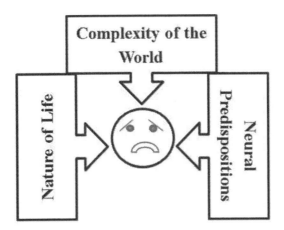

The Three Major Causes of Unhappiness

First is the *complexity of the world*. An unintended consequence of our material and technological prosperity is that we have collectively created a world where our brains must carry a much larger load of uncertainty than they were designed for. Most of us live our lives with dozens (if not hundreds) of user IDs and passwords to remember, countless undone tasks, more choices than our brains can process, and a deluge of news that constantly reminds us of the ugliest places human minds can go.

Second is the *nature of life*. We love control, but we don't have control. We don't get to pick some of the most important aspects of life—our parents, children, country of birth, race, sex, genetic makeup, and so much more. We all are transient visitors on this planet, yet we hate the idea of mortality. We want to protect our loved ones but cannot guarantee that our efforts will succeed. We can't predict the next moment, yet we want it to be favorable to us. The result is a mismatch between our expectations and reality, a mismatch that fashions angst and unhappiness.

The third source of unhappiness resides in our *neural predispositions*. Our ancestors had to make several compromises in their evolutionary struggle for survival. Our brains carry the resulting evolutionary baggage. A large body of research points at these eleven of our tendencies that push happiness away:

* Negativity bias: Most of us selectively attend to, believe, and inflate the negative. I believed the bully and the teacher because they fed this natural instinct of mine.

* Hedonic adaptation: We adapt to and discount the good that becomes familiar to us. Every fabulous toy I acquired, after a short period of excitement, lost novelty and allure. I was raised by loving parents and siblings in a warm home with enough food to eat and games to play, all of which I took for granted.

* Comparison: I compare what I have with what others have. Even if my possessions are adequate for my present needs, if others, particularly those I compete with, have more than I do, I get discontented and envious.

* Imaginary fears: For my brain, imaginary is real. I hurt myself more with imaginary fears than real happenings. Most of my medical self-diagnoses—multiple cancers, three heart attacks, two strokes, sudden death—I have experienced in my mind, not in my body.

* Emotional pain = physical pain: Emotional pain has hijacked the brain pathways that developed to handle physical pain. My brain thus can't tell the difference between emotional and physical pain. (In fact, in one research study, investigators found that paracetamol reduced emotional reactivity.)

* Mirror neurons: When I see others hurt, particularly those who are close to me, my own pain pathways activate. With the information from the remotest corners of the world accessible to us each day, ten minutes of watching the news could show us more pain than our ancestors saw in ten years.

* Short-term gratifications: I can't resist calorie-dense food, I enjoy being a couch potato rather than an exercise buff, and I struggle to keep my fantasies in check—my brain is addicted to short-term gratifications.

* Mental projection: I struggle with both being in the moment and having a long-term perspective. I project just about far enough to be miserable.

* Prediction errors: I am not good at predicting how I will respond to a particular experience, and I confuse *wanting* for *liking*. Once I acquire the things I seek for happiness, they either don't satisfy me or give pleasure only for a short time.

* Conflicted by nature: My brain is designed as a conflicted organ. It has fear and reward centers that pull it in different directions. It struggles with balancing short-term versus long-term goals and self versus others focus. My kidneys are not conflicted right now about their job, but my brain is. The inherent conflict between yielding to temptations (think donut) or exercising self-control creates significant load of uncertainty and thus stress.

* Wandering mind: To top it all, I spend most of my days allowing my mind to wander, lost in an internal monologue, detached from the real world.

Do you see how despite its awesomeness, our brain has some peculiarities that can multiply our suffering? Our brain was designed for survival and safety, not peace and happiness. We pay the price for this natural state in excessive angst, paranoia, and deficits in compassion and gratitude.

Coming back to my journey, as I learned about my brain and confessed to others about the noise in my head, I realized that I had company. Every single person I met struggled with this noise. At some point my quest to understand the problem shifted to the search for solutions. "While the complexity of the world and the nature of life are not in my direct influence, I might have better luck with influencing my neural predispositions," I thought.

First, I tried traditional contemplative practices, but they didn't satisfy me. I needed something more practical and easier to adapt to my life, which now included two kids, pagers, urgent e-mails, overnight calls, research-grant deadlines, mortgage payments, and a mound of junk mail. With time and effort, I got several lucky breaks and was able to formulate a structured approach to help myself and others. I describe the resulting programs and skills in my previous two books—*Mayo Clinic Guide to Stress-Free Living* and *Mayo Clinic Handbook for Happiness*.

While writing these two books and applying the ideas to my own life, I realized that if I want to be a good doctor, researcher, educator, and citizen, I must first become a good husband and a good father. That's the reason my title on the front page of this book reads HD, which stands for *husband and dad* (not *happiness doctor*, *human development*, *hard drive*, *Home Depot*, or *Harley-Davidson*, although these are all legitimate expansions of this abbreviation).

I feel I am at a better place today than I was one or two decades ago. But I still struggle with my ingrained predispositions. I try to think healthy and prosocial thoughts, avoid speaking harsh words, read the right books, and try my best not to do anything wrong, yet from some unguarded corner an unhealthy craving, fear, selfishness, or ego creeps in. I am far away from my concept of my ideal self. I believe my ongoing struggles come from two challenges—my mind's tendency to forget, and the difficulty I face in overriding my innate instincts. My mind needs constant reminders because it forgets the values I should be serving and embodying.

I believe I need the discipline to immerse myself in the higher values until they become such an integral part of my life that I become one with them. The Immerse Program is intended to help you and me immerse in these values.

If you feel you need some discipline to effect a positive change in your life, then join me. Together, we will strive to reach a point where deeper presence and higher values become natural to us, like breathing, and begin to provide us the peace and joy we are seeking.

Let me next share with you a few words about resilient living before I describe the steps of the Immerse Program.

What is Resilient Living?

*Y*our happiness, stress level, risk of depression and resilience are influenced by three interacting factors: your genes, circumstances, and the choices you make. Though the contribution of each of these factors varies in different studies, approximately half the variability in your happiness depends on a combination of genetic predisposition and life situations, with the rest half depending on the choices you make.

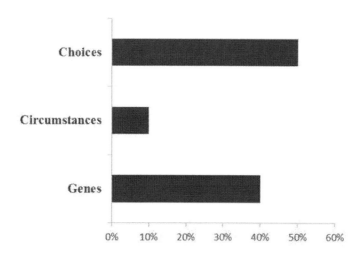

The Three Factors That Influence Your Wellbeing

While you have little control over your genes and the pace with which the world changes around you, you have incredible (and often untapped) ability to choose your thoughts, words and actions based on your highest ideals. Through exercising this option, you can live with resilience. "Immerse: A 52-Week Course in Resilient Living" is designed to help you in this process. Let's first understand what is resilience.

Whether it be coping with a loss, arguing with a teenager, recovering from an illness, dealing with a difficult client, or resisting a donut, you draw from a well of energy to negotiate the ups and downs of life. That energy is resilience. **Resilience is the core strength you use to lift the load of life.** Resilience helps you withstand adversity, bounce back from life's downturns and grow with each adversity. Resilience also helps you develop the foresight to prevent future adversity. Think of someone you personally know who you truly admire for his or her ability to withstand different challenges. How would you describe that person's positive attributes? I have asked this question of thousands of people. Here is the synthesis of the answers I have received. Resilient people:

* are emotionally strong.
* are kind, gentle and patient.
* are grateful for life's little and larger blessings.
* are compassionate even amid personal stress.
* are gracious in forgiving others.
* live a life of purpose.
* are filled with love and wisdom.
* live their days with intentionality and aren't quick to judge others.
* live for others.
* often have a strong anchor of faith.

Resilience has two core domains—Physical and Psycho-spiritual, with the latter having three components—cognitive, emotional and spiritual.

Physical resilience: Physically resilient people fall sick less often and recover quickly from an illness. Healthy diet, active lifestyle, adequate sleep, self care and good quality medical help, all contribute to physical resilience. While physical resilience contributes to overall resilience, you don't have to be in perfect health to be resilient. In fact, some of the most inspiring examples of resilience come from people struggling with serious medical conditions.

Cognitive resilience: Cognitive resilience is your ability to maintain focus, judgment, insight and decision making skills amid life's difficulties. Cognitively resilient people aren't just intelligent; they preserve their intelligence even when feeling overwhelmed. They are excellent at handling deadlines and are the last to buckle under pressure.

Emotional resilience: Emotional resilience is frequently experiencing positive emotions and recovering quickly from negative emotions. Emotionally resilient people are humble, kind, gentle, and patient, both toward others and themselves. They are flexible and are pragmatically optimistic. You'll generally find them calm and happy, and able to look at the bright side in an adverse situation. One of the single most important contributor to emotional resilience is personal experience with overcoming adversity through intentional actions.

Spiritual resilience: Spiritual resilience is your ability to maintain a higher meaning and altruistic perspective, both during happier and difficult times. Spiritually resilient people aren't limited by their mind's attraction to short-term gratification. They seek the good, not necessarily the pleasant. Their beliefs aren't shackled by burdensome dogmas. Instead, they use their positive beliefs to benefit the mankind. They see every human being as precious and are generous in gifting their compassion.

Through maximizing your potential in each of these four domains, emerges your individual resilience. Through our collective individual resilience emerges organizational resilience. Research shows that the greatest destroyer of organizational resilience are workplace conflicts / toxic workplace politics, constant demand resource imbalance, perceived lack of control and lack of meaning. Research also shows that the two greatest resource of individual resilience are: one's own inner strength and one's relationships. Hence enhancing individual resilience, improving workplace camaraderie, optimizing demand with resources, and providing control and meaning, are the key elements that can enhance organizational resilience.

Resilient organizations create resilient societies, resilient nations and ultimately resilient world. In this book, my focus will be on practices to enhance your individual cognitive, emotional and spiritual resilience, that I believe will feed into the larger purpose.

Resilient living is bringing these insights to your daily life and thus choose to live a life with courage and meaning. I like to define resilient living as *living with intentionality, deeper presence, contentment, and kindness.* Let's talk about each of these aspects.

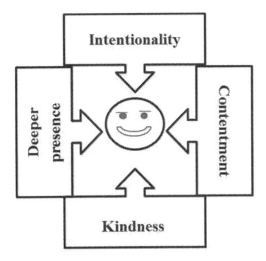

The Four Core Components of Resilient Living

Intentionality

Most animals spend their entire life driven by instincts and habits—a state of automaticity. In humans, automaticity traps us in the allure of short-term gratifications, the dread of imaginary fears, and the cobweb of ordinary ruminations, all fashioned by incessant mind wanderings. Living with an instinct-driven, automatic mind is like driving a car without holding the steering wheel. Such a car is bound to wander off its lane, onto the rumble strip, and eventually into the ditch. If you wish to govern your life with conscious choices, you'll need to break free of this automaticity—by cultivating intentionality.

Intentionality means taking charge by becoming an active participant in the flow of life. At a restaurant, you don't tell the waiter to just get whatever. You carefully pick the food that best matches your palate and wallet. Similarly, intentional living involves carefully choosing your thoughts, words, and actions.

Intentionality helps you maximally use the phenomenal thinking power of your brain. An intentional mind thinks about life's meaning and aligns the short-term actions with this long-term meaning. Such a mind is disciplined, virtuous, engaged, and filled with hope and possibilities. It chooses to think thoughts, speak words, and engage in life's pursuits based on timeless values.

The three most important skills that can help you strengthen intentionality are deeper presence, contentment, and kindness.

Deeper presence

Our innate presence is superficial and partial because of fragmented and weak attention. During most conscious moments, we have two planes of presence—one in which we are doing and one in which we are thinking. Lack of congruence between physical and psychological presence blocks authentic, undistracted engagement with life.

Just as drillers dig a deeper well to access the water table or oil, to access the well of wisdom you need to fashion a deeper presence by strong attention. With such presence, you start seeing patterns in a random landscape. You appreciate details you hadn't seen before. Your error rate goes down. You learn to discern complexity more easily. You become less reactive. When you immerse fully in life, your entire day becomes a 'flow' experience.

You need deeper presence in order to fully engage with the people you connect with each day. An undistracted caring presence can be tremendously healing to both the giver and the receiver. Loving relationships, lasting friendships, professional partnerships, creative pursuits—you cannot achieve excellence in any of these without deeper presence.

Such presence isn't innate to most of us, and it requires effort to cultivate. The good news is that with effort, you build capacity, so with time, your innate attention becomes stronger, translating into spontaneous deep presence.

Your deeper, authentic, undistracted presence gifts you with a fuller life driven by your core values of contentment and kindness.

Contentment

Contentment is a deep feeling of fulfillment that emerges from the daily practice of gratitude. As we advance emotionally and spiritually, we pass through three phases with respect to contentment.

Phase I: Lack of Contentment. In this phase we strive for the world's attention and busy ourselves collecting toys to thwart boredom and help us climb on the social totem pole. A proportion of us close our life's book after having climbed barely a few rungs on this ladder. With so many rungs still unscaled, we experience only occasional sprinkles of contentment.

We don't realize that the game we are playing is rigged. Our mind's expectations and desires naturally stay a step ahead of our accomplishments—a state of programmed dissatisfaction. Relying on our mind's natural state to find contentment is a recipe for failure.

Phase II: Contentment. Those who realize the above wisdom, amid their striving, dig deeper. They discover and taste the delicacy of gratitude and acceptance. Contentment naturally follows. Contentment provides them respite and fresh energy. It frees their attention so they can focus on living a meaning-filled life through enhancing the well-being of their fellow travelers.

The state of contentment slowly progresses to the third phase, which curiously again brings discontent. This time, however, the discontent is different, and it signifies real progress.

Phase III: Contentment with Dissatisfaction. People in this third phase are dissatisfied because even though they are content with their accomplishments and possessions, they can't accept the status quo of the world—with countless beings experiencing unimaginable pain and suffering. They want to help and are passionate about making the world a happier and kinder place. They aren't content with their own comforts. They wish to share their peace and joy with others. They create transformations through inventions, expeditions, revolutions, and more. They strive to decrease suffering.

Such striving is anchored by humility and powered by compassion. Lack of contentment now provides energy, tremendously increases social awareness, and fuels passion. An invariable accompaniment of this discontent is kindness.

Kindness

World over, the single most desirable trait in your partner, friend, parent, teacher, neighbor, colleague, or child is kindness. Kindness is the daily practice of compassion. Kindness has countless expressions. Patience with someone who seems slower than usual; forgiveness for the waiter who spilled water on your shirt; the ability to provide a loving, gentle presence at home; lack of judgment toward someone who looks different; humility in accomplishments; the ability to speak softly even in argument—all are different expressions of kindness.

Kindness isn't easy to consistently embody. It takes superhuman effort to remain kind while experiencing personal adversity, unkind treatment, stress, or anger. It is in these situations, however, that kindness is most needed.

A kind anchor provides the much-needed self-control and clarity of thinking that will prevent an argument from breaking a relationship. For example, if you are committed to kindness, even if your partner is snappy one evening, you won't immediately react. The clarity of thinking that kindness provides will help you exercise self-control so you can look past his or her reactivity. Such kindness needs practice. Just as a tree doesn't strengthen its roots the night of the storm, you can't develop kindness overnight; you'll have to practice it in the littlest experiences—to the moth visiting your home, the telemarketer who trespasses into your peace, and the airline agent who botches your flight booking. With practice, you'll become instinctively kind; kindness will become effortless and will require no active thought.

When your primordial instinct becomes that of kindness, you start gifting your kindness to everyone you touch. This change transforms your life. You create your own little heaven that walks with you wherever you go.

Come, let's immerse ourselves in the journey that'll take us there.

How to Use This Book

Through this book and the accompanying program, I'll walk with you on a one-year journey into resilient living. In this journey we will together embrace deeper presence, live our days guided by our core values, and make our best effort to become the kindest and most grateful person we can be. The emphasis is on practice. Any reflection, science, or philosophy I offer is guided to support a daily practice. You can engage with the book in two ways:

1. Read it as a traditional book.
2. Use the book concurrently with the online Immerse program.

The first option is self explanatory. I will next share some details of how to engage with the online program. Engaging with the program is likely to give you the full benefit of the book. You can participate in the program in three steps.

Step	When	What	Description
I	Now	52-week commitment	Read and sign the commitment page and make a promise to yourself that you'll live the next fifty-two weeks with the highest values and the deepest presence.

Step	When	What	Description
II	Week 0	IIa. Assess	Assess your current level of presence, gratitude (contentment), and kindness (compassion) using the PGK scale (look below).
		IIb. Watch	Watch these three videos on YouTube: 1. A Very Happy Brain (Animation) https://www.youtube.com/watch?v=GZZ0zpUQhBQ 2. Happy Brain (TEDx presentation) https://www.youtube.com/watch?v=KZIGekgoaz4 3. The 5-3-2 Plan https://www.youtube.com/watch?v=-BfOuaXz2lU You can find all of these (and additional) videos on the home page of the website Stressfree.org. Pick one or two practices you learned from the TEDx talk and the 5-3-2 Plan, and apply the practices to your daily life.
		IIc. Connect	Most days I'll post a tweet or a blog with a thought aligned with the daily practice. If you wish, please connect using my Twitter account, @amitsoodmd. Also access the practices on this web link: Stressfree.org/Immerse/.

Step	When	What	Description
III	Weeks 1-52	Immerse	Now you're ready to immerse in the resilient-living program. The program has two components: Insights and Practices. * Insights - Each week the program offers two fresh insights, often shared as stories, by synthesizing ideas from science, philosophy and daily life experiences. If the insights suggested for the week do not resonate with you, then you're welcome to pick different insights from the book or look for additional ideas elsewhere. * Practices - Aligned with each insight, the book provides one suggested daily practice. Additional practices are available at Stressfree.org/Immerse. You can pick the practice/s suggested in the book or online, or create your own practice/s that better suit to your personal situation. Further, you can choose the number of days in a week you wish to practice the program. Although the practices are arranged by weeks they are not incremental. So you can join the online program anytime at the current active week.
Optional (anytime)			Consider reading one of the following two books: *Mayo Clinic Guide to Stress-Free Living* or *Mayo Clinic Handbook for Happiness*.

Step I

52 - Week Commitment

I, _____, make a
commitment to myself to live the next fifty-two weeks of my life with deeper
presence and the highest values. During this time, I will make a concerted
effort to be the kindest and most grateful person I can be.

Signed _____

Dated _____

Step II

✿

Assess, Watch, Connect

❋ Self-Assessment (Step IIa)

Before we embark on this journey together, let's first assess where we are at the starting point. Carefully read the descriptions below and circle the one that most closely describes you for presence, gratitude and kindness (The PGK Scale).

The PGK Scale for Self-assessment of Presence, Gratitude and Kindness			
Attribute	Description: Which of the following best describes your state of mind in the previous 24 hours.* Please make sure to score your <u>lived experience</u> and not what you believe in or intended.		**Score**
1. Presence	In the previous 24 hours…	I was extremely distracted.	1
		I was able to focus but got easily distracted.	2
		I was able to focus and did not get easily distracted.	3
		I was able to focus, did not get easily distracted, and often looked at others with kindness.	4
		I consistently had undistracted, kind, non-judgmental presence.	5
2. Gratitude	In the previous 24 hours…	I was not grateful for anything or anyone.	1
		I was only grateful for big achievements and/or people who went out of their way to help me.	2
		I was grateful for small daily pleasures.	3
		I needed nothing external to feel grateful.	4
		I was grateful even for adversities and losses.	5
3. Kindness	In the previous 24 hours…	I was not kind to anyone.	1
		I was only kind to those from whom I could benefit.	2
		I was kind to everyone as long as I felt well, physically and emotionally.	3
		I was kind to everyone even when I did not feel well.	4
		I was kind to even those who may not be my well-wishers or may have hurt me.	5

* You can also pick a different time frame, such as 72 hours or a week.

You get a three digit score for PGK, in that sequence. For example if you selected 2 for presence, 2 for gratitude and 3 for kindness, then your score is – P2G2K3. It gives you an idea where you are and in which aspects you can improve.

I am confident your score wasn't 111, nor was it 555. Most of us start off in some combinations of 2s and 3s. That is just fine. Our goal will be to frequently assess where we are with this score, and hopefully move upward as our practice matures.

Set an intention to improve your PGK score for today. For example, if you scored P2G2K3, and wish to enhance your gratitude (so your score is P2G3K3), then try to savor and be grateful for small pleasures of the day. My hope is that eventually your score is consistently P4G4K4, with days when you even touch 5, at least with gratitude and kindness.

✻ *Watch* (Step II b)

In this step I invite you to watch three videos.

The first video, A Very Happy Brain, is a five-minute animation that synthesizes some of the evidence from neurosciences to help us understand how our brain processes pain and suffering and why the practice of gratitude and compassion can help us decrease our pain.

https://www.youtube.com/watch?v=GZZ0zpUQhBQ

The second video, Happy Brain, is an eighteen-minute TEDx presentation, that expands on the science shared in the first video and offers practical solutions that you can implement in your life to lower your stress and enhance wellbeing and happiness.

https://www.youtube.com/watch?v=KZIGekgoaz4

The third video, the 5-3-2 plan, in one minute and fifteen seconds, provides you a reminder of the three core practices in the SMART (Stress Management and Resiliency Training) program (Look at the end of the book if you want more information about the SMART program). It invites you to send silent gratitude first thing in the morning to <u>five</u> people who make you happy, meet your family at the end of the day for at least <u>three</u> minutes as your long-lost friend with no desire to 'improve' them, and when seeing other people, for the first <u>two</u> seconds send them a silent good wish.

https://www.youtube.com/watch?v=-BfOuaXz2lU

You can find all of these (and additional) videos on the home page of the website Stressfree.org.

Once you are familiar with the basic construct of the program, I invite you to commit to one practice for the next one week. Assess your progress at the end of the week and find ways to deepen your practice. The two most popular practices are the morning gratitude and the three minute rule. If you wish to learn more about these and other practices and the entire construct of the SMART program, you are welcome to look for Mayo Clinic books on Stress-Free Living and Happiness.

* *Connect* (Step II c)

I am committed to embody one or the other practice for each day of my life. I will share with you how my practice is going via social media (Twitter account @amitsoodmd). You can find additional suggested practices for the week on the website Stressfree.org/Immerse/. I invite you to explore and connect with these online assets.

The goal is for you to surround yourself with, and thus immerse in thoughts related to the higher values.

Now we are ready to begin the third and final step – Immerse.

Step III

Immerse

*I*mmerse is designed in a way so that you don't have to read or practice in any particular order. Each insight and practice is independent and not necessarily incremental to the previous insight or practice. If, however, you wish to work along with me, then join the online program at the current week.

Week 1

During this week you'll anchor in your primary identity—that of a kind human being—and lift your self-esteem by choosing whom to believe and whom not to.

1. My Singing

Anchor in your primary identity.

Dear friend,

I had no idea how bad a singer I am until one day, while I was singing, my daughter started crying. She was crying <u>because</u> of how badly I was singing! (This is called the Dunning-Kruger effect—an illusion some unskilled people carry that they are very talented. I am sure you know a few of them!)

First I was a little confused, next I found it hilarious, and then we all burst out laughing. Now this has become a family joke—I deliberately sing worse than my innate abilities, and she fake cries louder than her natural sobs.

My ability to accept her rejection, find humor in it, and turn it around into a celebratory moment depended on how much my self-worth hinged on her perception of my singing talent. If my primary identity were a singer, then it would be a much bigger deal. If not, then I could flow with the tiny slight.

Singing is just one attribute; there are many aspects of life where I might get an F, likely some that I don't even know. While my daughter's emotional expression could be considered cute and funny, I certainly do not wish to cause real anguish because of my inadequacies. I should continue to examine myself and welcome well-meaning feedback.

I need to carefully choose the attributes I allow to influence my self-worth. My primary identity should be that of a kind human being. I should let nothing tarnish that identity.

I should peg my worthiness on my core intentions and not the outcome of my actions; on my effort and not the result; on the meaning I serve and not the (dollar) reward society provides; and on my ability to help and serve and not my physical attributes. With this mind-set, I will open myself to critique, learn from negative feedback, and turn those moments into memorable celebratory events while growing not despite but because of them.

Maybe I will then have the courage and energy to work on my singing and actually make my daughter cry from the depth of my melody. If you present this possibility to her today, she is likely to roll her eyes and say, "That ain't happenin', mister!"

May you sing the song of your heart each day, no matter your ability to sing.

Take care.

Amit

* Suggested practice: Today, I will give a heartfelt compliment to at least one person who I know seldom receives compliments. (For additional practices, visit Stressfree.org/Immerse/)

2. Self-Belief

Whom not to believe

Dear friend,

In a recent study, one out of every two girls avoided activities such as swimming and other sports because of body-image issues, and one out of four girls was afraid to raise her hand in class. So many of us miss out on precious opportunities because we feel inadequate and afraid to speak up. Prevalence of low self-esteem is difficult to precisely measure in the population, but it is likely high. Estimates range from 20 to 80 percent.

I struggle with the same challenge. On most days I could use a pat on the back. When I am left to myself, my self-esteem starts to dip. I get depleted until something lifts me up—a kind e-mail, a warm hello, an authentic smile, a well-meaning text, or any other packet of energy that reminds me that I matter and am worthy.

That doesn't happen every day. And of course there are days when I encounter more than one instance that makes me feel relatively worthless.

I used to get annoyed and irritated by these occurrences. Later, as I matured, I started focusing on the message and not the messenger. I used the feedback as an opportunity for growth.

However, I have learned that unfortunately there are instances when the negative feedback comes from a place of ignorance. It isn't a well-meaning critique. The harsh words are meant to be vicious and are not designed to help. I watch for three signs to reach this conclusion—first, when the person doesn't deliver the feedback with kind words; second, when the person focuses on me rather than the situation; and third, when the feedback doesn't offer a solution or hope for a solution.

I would love to keep learning with each experience. But I am human. There are times when I choose not to learn and instead tell myself I will not believe in a person who doesn't believe in me.

May you be brave, strong, and kind and give no one permission to lower your self-worth.

Take care.

Amit

*   Suggested practice: Today, I will not doubt my capabilities.
    (For additional practices, visit Stressfree.org/Immerse/)

Week 2

*D*uring this week you'll heal your relationships by bringing greater wisdom and love into your life, and you'll begin to create a world where greed is rare and fear isn't necessary.

3. Relationships

A lesson from Pearl Harbor

Dear friend,

In December 1941 the world witnessed the attack on Pearl Harbor which was followed, in August 1945, by the destructive forces of the atomic bomb. The United States and Japan engaged in a most tragic war in this time period.

Fast-forward a few decades, and the two countries now count each other as strong allies. You couldn't have predicted in August 1945 that in just a few decades, the United States and Japan would become the strongest trade partners. Currently Japan ranks number four in its trade relations with the United States, after Canada, China, and Mexico. With the changing times, circumstances change, and so do relationships.

Bring this wisdom to your personal life. An unfortunate event may have pulled you apart from someone you were close to. That event could have been circumstantial or even intentional. However, with the changing times, realities change, and so do perceptions. Perhaps you are more mature now. Perhaps the other person is more mature now. Perhaps there is a real possibility of forgiveness. Perhaps you can find meaning in healing the relationship before you both close your life.

Recognize that the previous-you and the previous-others were different beings from those existing today. Do not let the present-you and the future-you be limited by the previous-you. Find a path toward healing your relationships by bringing greater wisdom and love into your life, and through wisdom and love, greater kindness, acceptance, and meaning.

If forgiveness seems too remote and unrealistic today, consider gratitude for what is right in the other person and compassion for the collective human suffering. Gratitude and compassion together might clear the path for acceptance and forgiveness to find home in you.

May your world thrive in peace; may that peace come through you.

Take care.

Amit

* Suggested practice: Today, I will send a silent good wish to at least one person who annoys me.
  (For additional practices, visit Stressfree.org/Immerse/)

4. Selflessness

True paradigm shift

Dear friend,

An animal existence revolves around eating, keeping from being eaten, and reproducing—appetitive, defensive, and reproductive pressures. Each of these forces enhances the self by protecting it or attracting energy toward it. Within limits, this is appropriate and essential for survival.

But one species on our planet has chosen otherwise. It is willing to let go of personal gains by enhancing the collective. It opens its chest to take the hurts and protect others. It considers forgiveness a marker of strength, not weakness. We are that species.

This is a true paradigm shift—living to give out (and not pull) energy. We humans have fundamentally changed the definition of a good life. According to us, a good life is not one that marinates in greed and selfish wants; it is a meaning-filled life lush with gratitude and compassion. In the altruistic moments of gratitude and compassion, you forget self-interest. In those moments, you find freedom.

On a day you feel despondent from the headline news, look at the work of a few Nobel Peace Prize winners. It will uplift you and give you hope. No other species on our planet has created selfless beings consciously choosing a life devoted to helping others. Many scientists believe altruistic behavior in most animals is governed by instincts; it is not a conscious choice. Not so for us.

We need to accelerate this revolution and build a world where greed is rare and fear isn't necessary. In that world, compassion will be the dominating force guiding our conscious choices. I am certain the children in that world will be very happy. Let's work together to create a world where honesty doesn't surprise anyone and where every person's life is a testament of the virtues.

May you live in a world where kindness and selflessness are the norm; may you help create such a world.

Take care.

Amit

* Suggested practice: Today, I will work without thinking about who gets the credit.
(For additional practices, visit Stressfree.org/Immerse/)

Week 3

During this week you'll practice delaying judgment of others by assuming positive intent, and you'll also develop the healthy habit of being able to laugh at yourself.

5. Softening Judgments

If you have to assume...

Dear friend,

No one exists in isolation. If you remove me from my context, I'll lose most of my meaning. I also provide context for others who find meaning from me. My identity thus is meaningless without reference to everything that surrounds me, including my past. If you judge me out of my context, you might miss the whole point.

I was judgmental when I heard about a fifteen-year-old girl who decided to get married to her high-school sweetheart. I was embarrassed about my premature judgment when I learned that the girl had a terminal illness and wanted the experience of becoming a bride before she passed away.

A single note of a piano may mean nothing in isolation, while the same note might fit very well within the concerto. I have learned that I shouldn't judge others out of their context.

But how often do I know their full context? Most people don't feel safe or comfortable sharing their full context. Why not then quit judging and use the energy so saved to do something meaningful?

I could take it to the next level. Instead of negative judgment, I could instill positive assumptions. I love to be trusted, to get the benefit of doubt. Why not give the same gift to others?

I shouldn't trash the book if I can't make sense of the story after reading just one page. I should recognize that in all likelihood this page fits perfectly in the story. It's just that I haven't read the complete story. Most likely, I won't ever get a chance to read the book (others' stories) from cover to cover. So I should just assume positive intent. Period.

May you live in a world that accepts and embraces you for who you are.

Take care.

Amit

* Suggested practice: Today, I will assume that most people around me have good intentions.
(For additional practices, visit Stressfree.org/Immerse/)

6. Laughter

❧❧

A good laugh

Dear friend,

Laughter evolved to defuse tension, improve social connection, and create bonding. When we laugh with others, we send the message, "I like you, and I am willing to play with you." Hearts that laugh together, beat together.

Research shows laughter provides a good physical workout, generates mental relaxation, lowers blood pressure and pain, and even improves immunity. You're thirty times more likely to laugh in good company than alone. Further, the more you laugh *with* others rather than *at* someone, the greater the health benefit.

I like to laugh with others. I am embarrassed to accept that I have also sometimes laughed *at* others. I have noticed irrationality and silly mistakes in others and have laughed at those. Yet I don't like anyone laughing at me.

I have a choice. I could be stiff and defensive. I could thwart any attempt of others to laugh at me. Or I could learn to laugh at myself. I believe the latter is a healthier option.

When I laugh at myself, I get the same kick that I do when laughing at others. I am entertained without being unkind. It keeps me humble. It improves my relationships.

Laughing at myself thus is a true win-win situation. It expresses humility. I should learn to laugh at myself more often.

I should also make it a habit to laugh with and not laugh at. If I surround myself with kind, well-meaning people whom I love and trust, I will laugh more, and laugh more healthfully. In order to do that, I should become a person whom people love, trust, and feel safe to laugh with.

May love and laughter fill each corner of your home, today and forever.

Take care.

Amit

*   Suggested practice: Today, I will be willing to laugh at my past mistakes.
(For additional practices, visit Stressfree.org/Immerse/)

Week 4

During this week you'll try to embrace the imperfections that surround you by finding meaning in them, and you'll minimize revisiting hurtful memories.

7. Accepting Imperfections

Can a perfect world remain perfect?

Dear friend,

Let's think about what it might mean to have a perfect world.

This will be a world with plenty of resources, no natural disasters, and no crime. No one will fall sick in this world; there will be no disease, no premature death, and a very long life span. I can assure you of one thing—citizens of this world will be very miserable. Let me explain why.

Our mind gets used to all that is right and desirable, a phenomenon called hedonic adaptation. When was the last time you were truly grateful for the fresh feeling in your mouth after brushing your teeth or the comfort of the elevator at your workplace? People living in a perfect world will quickly become used to, and thus oblivious of, its perfection. They will then ask the question, what next?

Our greater excitement doesn't come from getting; it comes from trying and anticipating. The experience of struggling and then overcoming is uniquely pleasurable, much more so than succeeding with no challenges. Losing a game of chess while playing a stronger opponent is more enjoyable than winning while playing a much weaker opponent.

In a world with no struggles and no suffering, there will be no need for compassion. With no flaws and no hurts, our minds might lose capacity for acceptance and forgiveness. The greatest loss will likely be of meaning. With nothing to improve, no one to save, and no adversity to overcome, people might not know what to do with their days. They might revert to all kinds of addictions, eventually making their perfect world imperfect. Then they might go about improving their world and thus eventually find happiness.

Our neural system hasn't adapted for a perfect world. We need the world's imperfections. They inspire us to improve ourselves, cultivate compassion and forgiveness, and find meaning so we can rise above our limitations.

Personally, I wouldn't mind a world that was a little less imperfect but that had just about enough struggles to keep us going, to cause us to be compassionate and help us find meaning without getting numb to and petrified by the atrocities we see these days. Until we arrive at that Goldilocks state, for which we should strive, consider that our world's imperfections steer us toward greater personal perfection. The imperfections that surround us help us grow. Accept them and find meaning in working with them.

May you face fewer imperfections; may no one demand perfection from you.

Take care.

Amit

* Suggested practice: Today, I will truly try to see others from within their perspective, with an intention to validate them.
(For additional practices, visit Stressfree.org/Immerse/)

8. Lessons from a Cough

Working with old memories

Dear friend,

I saw a mother and her little girl sitting in an airport lounge. The little girl was unwell; she was constantly coughing. Her mother wasn't sure how to help her child, other than by hugging her, giving her sips of water, and patting her back so she could fall asleep. Sleep finally arrived; the coughing went down but didn't completely disappear.

Coughing helps keep the passageways into the lungs clear of any debris. As our species prioritized speaking (phonation) above smelling (olfaction), our voice box moved closer to the food pipe. This increased the risk of food entering the lung passages, leading to the evolution of the cough. A cough that dislodges foreign bodies can save a life.

However, there is a second form of cough, a dry, hacking, annoying cough in response to chemical or inflammatory irritation of the airways, like the little girl was experiencing. We all have tried to suppress it at some point. This cough is often unhelpful and can be very frustrating and fatiguing. Excessive chronic cough can even hurt, by producing rib fractures, air leakage in the lungs, hernias, increased eye pressure, and even loss of consciousness.

In my medical career, I have seen thousands of patients with a cough. The majority of us experience this second type of cough—a true nuisance. Cough is one of nature's protective reflexes that hurts too many to protect a few. Our negative thoughts and ruminations about previous hurts are similar.

While occasionally harboring the hurts and thinking about them might help, more commonly, such thoughts injure us and multiply our misery. This is because when we remember a hurt, we reexperience it. And when we reexperience it, we strengthen it further.

When revisiting a hurtful thought, ask yourself, is this thought serving a purpose? If it's helpful and protective, find meaning in that thought, keep it with you, and help it direct your self-protective actions.

If it's unhelpful, find ways to avoid visiting it, by taking your attention elsewhere or reinterpreting the thought with one of the higher principles (gratitude, compassion, acceptance, meaning, forgiveness), so it loses its sharp sting.

May your thoughts be happy, healthy, healed, and hope-filled; may you help others think such thoughts.

Take care.

Amit

*   Suggested practice: Today, I will think of a good memory each time my mind takes me to a hurtful one.
    (For additional practices, visit Stressfree.org/Immerse/)

Week 5

During this week you'll try to befriend your worries and look at others and your world with fresh eyes (perspective).

9. Worries

The right worries

Dear friend,

On most days I struggle with one or more worries. I worry because I have preferences. I worry because I wish my world to be safer. I worry because I can imagine adversity and would like to prevent it. I worry because I am human and I care.

Any species that raises children and has intellect, imagination, and preferences is bound to worry. My mind believes that my worries might secure my own and others' safety. My mind isn't wrong. Specific worries about specific issues with a focus on the probable and on finding solutions have helped me many times. But worrying just because I should worry hasn't helped me.

Worry that motivates is useful; worry that paralyzes isn't. Beyond a threshold, worry becomes toxic and paralyzing. I have worried to the point of losing my ability to think clearly.

I can't give up worrying. I don't wish to. Instead, I should harness my worries. I should try to understand the logic behind my worries and, when appropriate, seek help from others. I should only worry about the issues that are worry-worthy—where the price I pay for worrying is worth the benefit. My worries should only concern possibilities that can realistically happen. While it is possible that a hippopotamus could jump out of an aircraft above our home and crash through our ceiling, the chances of that happening are quite low. I shouldn't worry about that.

Finally, my worries should focus on those problems for which actions can make a difference.

With these qualifiers, worry is a friend that looks out for me. Without these qualifiers, worry is a buzz in my head that interferes with the music of my life.

May you have fewer worries; may you swap your worries for hope, courage, and grit.

Take care.

Amit

* Suggested practice: Today, I will look for the logic behind my worries and will shed illogical worries.
  (For additional practices, visit Stressfree.org/Immerse/)

10. A Different World

You can live in a different world by changing how you look at your familiar world.

Dear friend,

Raised inner eyebrows and high cheekbones—our brain uses these two signs to decide whether a face is trustworthy. And we decide that in about thirty milliseconds—before we can even recognize whom that face belongs to.

Until very recently, external injury (inflicted by other humans, animals, or nature) was the most common cause of death. As a result, our ancestors defaulted to eyeing their world with suspicion. We thus have a scanner inside our head that constantly sizes people for threat and safety. Several researchers have found that when we look at someone who we think belongs to the "out" group, our amygdala (part of the fear center) activates. This instinct is useful when making quick judgments in an unsafe neighborhood. However, if this software defaults to being always on, then you seldom *truly* see anyone.

I suggest two potentially healthier alternatives. First, you can look at fellow human beings with an intention to send them a silent good wish (blessing), recognizing that everyone has struggles. No matter how successful or happy a person looks, he or she struggles with inner vulnerability, fear of losses, and regrets about a past action or inaction. You don't need to know the specifics to send your silent good wish.

Second, you can choose to remember that to someone in the world, the person in front of you is worth trillions of dollars—in other words, he or she is priceless. Recognizing the infinite value of each individual, you honor that person. You look at others with the eyes of the people who admire or adore them the most.

If you can consistently suffuse your eyes with kindness, then each time you see a person, it will seem as if you're seeing a friend or loved one. This will boost your well-being and connect you with a world that you wouldn't have otherwise known existed.

You have a choice—to look at the people in the world with suspicion or kindness. If you let your ancestral predisposition stay with you all the time, you'll look at the world with suspicion. Instead, when you feel safe, choose to look at others with kindness. The more you look at others with kindness, the more kindness you will find. Once you change how you look at your world, you'll change your world.

May you love the world you live in; may the world you live in love you.

Take care.

Amit

*   Suggested practice: Today, I will remember that each person I meet is priceless to someone.
    (For additional practices, visit Stressfree.org/Immerse/)

Week 6

*D*uring this week you'll be intentional about counting your blessings, and you'll develop a healthier connection with others by recognizing their priorities and honoring their constraints.

11. Count Your Blessings

What is as important as being blessed?

Dear friend,

During a flight I saw a child inconsolably crying; she had been denied a second lollipop. Her dad, keeping her in his lap, was valiantly using his work-in-progress skills. He seemed patient and kind, but no matter his efforts, he wasn't successful in soothing her. Her world had turned upside down at the prospect of a frustrated reward that she claimed to be rightfully hers.

I looked at the child thinking, "If only this little girl knew how fortunate she is." She was not among the 150 million orphaned children or the billion souls with no access to clean water. She was not among hundreds of millions of children who were born into poverty, who have a disability, or who are habitually abused. Her parents seemed to be nice people who cared for her. Until she learns not to fixate on a denied second lollipop and develops a more mature brain, however, she won't understand any of this.

We grown-ups aren't too dissimilar. We forget the million different blessings and anchor our present emotions on some little reward. We lose the big picture. I think it's a great loss.

It doesn't have to be this way. If you can see, hear, and walk; have a roof above your head; live in a warm home; and have access to clean water and food, you are better off than billions of people. You can choose to remember and be grateful for these blessings. Remembering your blessings will multiply them.

May you remember your infinite blessings; may you decorate your blessings with gratitude.

Take care.

Amit

* Suggested practice: Today, I will feel extra grateful for the food available to me.
  (For additional practices, visit Stressfree.org/Immerse/)

12. It's Up to Us

Soften your biases and invite values.

Dear friend,

Max, a fourth grader, is standing in the principal's office with his head down. He just hit a classmate in the face. He knows the drill.

But who is to blame? Is Max the one to blame? Did he fail us, or did we fail him? This is the fourth time in as many weeks he has erupted.

Instead of Max, should we blame his elder brother, Johnny, a seventh grader, who tied him up last night and beat him with a stick? But Johnny was only passing the buck for the frequent spankings he gets from his mother, Joanne. She gave birth to Johnny a few months before she turned nineteen, and she never again went to college.

Perhaps Joanne isn't the one to blame, either. Her family disowned her after she ran away with Rick. Now with three kids, she has to endure Rick's daily rants after he gets drunk. He has thrown her off the bed twice in the last month while spewing curse words. But Rick has his own reasons. When he was two, his mother abandoned him to the care of her husband, who was coping with PTSD, which he eventually took out on Rick.

We could keep climbing generations to find where it all started and how the vitriol of toxic emotions and hurts got passed around. I don't know whom to fault—perhaps nobody, perhaps everybody. But no matter the fault, it is up to us to look for answers.

Wherever you are right now, consider yourself a source of energy. What is the nature of the energy you are giving out, right at this moment? Are you mostly lost in thoughts and not giving much? Are you processing irritation, anger, and hurt? Or are you making an active effort to radiate loving energy, with kind and well-meaning thoughts, words, and actions? The energy you emanate starts a chain reaction. You get to choose the kind of reaction you start.

Instead of harshly judging others, if you choose to give out the energy of gratitude and compassion today in your microcosm, others will get it. With the change in you, you might eventually change the future for Max, Johnny, and countless others, even those who seem distant and disconnected.

The world desperately needs your loving energy. Little Max surely does, because one day he will have Max Juniors, and we don't want them standing in the principal's office with their head low.

It's up to us and nobody else.

May you never be harsh in judging others; may you never be judged harshly.

Take care.

Amit

* Suggested practice: Today, I will try to understand, from within his or her perspective, at least one person who seems unreasonable. (For additional practices, visit Stressfree.org/Immerse/)

Week 7

*D*uring this week you'll develop a more mature sense of self and nurture healthier desires so you seek, not out of greed, but for what you truly need and deserve.

13. Self-Worth

Secure sense of self

Dear friend,

Your self-worth is the intrinsic value you assign to yourself. You can't estimate your self-worth by comparing yourself with others. It has little to do with your accomplishments or the value that society places on you or your work. Your precise self-worth actually cannot be measured, since it is priceless. You can get the best estimate by asking a person who loves you unconditionally how much they value you. The answer would likely be trillions of dollars, if not more.

Don't use this realization to become haughty and arrogant. Instead, understand that you don't have to prove yourself to anybody; you are intrinsically priceless, and it's just fine to be humble and live a life serving a prosocial meaning, however simple that meaning might be.

We, however, don't live with these thoughts. We let inappropriate evaluation of the self—both by us and others—define our self-worth.

We often value ourselves based on the outcomes of our actions, not our intentions or efforts. Since the outcomes are unpredictable and context dependent, our self-perception isn't anchored and strong. It changes day by day, in step with our latest failure or success.

Others value us based on their ideals, the part of us they see, and their perception of how much we value them. Further, people are often better at critiquing than complimenting. The web gets even more complex when we receive mixed feedback from different people, sometimes with the same person changing his or her opinion in short order.

Do you see how your self-worth could be forever shifting, affecting your mood, the way you treat others, and your productivity?

I have learned the following lessons:

* I should remember that I am priceless, just like everyone else is.
* If I have to judge myself, I should look at my intentions and efforts and not at the outcome or dollar rewards.

* I should use every bit of well-meaning feedback (positive or negative) to become a better person.

* I should be liberal in providing well-deserved positive feedback to others.

Perhaps with this approach I will have a more secure sense of self, which might prompt me to help others feel the same. The world will transform when all of us wake up in the morning and tell our reflection in the mirror, "You are a good human being; you are priceless." Live your day remembering this fact and help others feel the same.

May you remind others that they are priceless; may others remind you that you are priceless.

Take care.

Amit

* Suggested practice: Today, I will judge myself not by my net worth but by the number of people I am (or was) able to help. (For additional practices, visit Stressfree.org/Immerse/)

14. Desire What You Deserve

What is a more realistic seeking?

Dear friend,

I should ask for what I genuinely deserve. I don't deserve a life free of adversity. With a third of my fellow citizens experiencing chronic pain and half likely to develop cancer, I shouldn't expect a pain-free, loss-free existence. It is more reasonable to request greater courage and wisdom so I can better face adversity.

Courage is your willingness to confront pain with strength, so moments of adversity become memories of glory. Courage weakens the grip of suffering, provides a source of focus and vitality, and multiplies willpower—all attributes that harness adversity to create an engine for growth. Such courage is a choice accessible to all of us. You're more likely to exercise this choice if you can find meaning in the adversity, through wisdom.

Wisdom is the capacity for right judgment. It is much more than knowledge. It is a combination of knowledge, experience, deeper insight, and compassion. In my pain, wisdom might discover a life-affirming meaning that could numb the pain. Within the losses, wisdom might find gains that make the losses look smaller.

When I ask for what I can't get or don't deserve, I degrade the value of my asking. I also embarrass the giver. If I truly believe that my desires influence what comes to me, I should seek wisdom and courage, not freedom from pain and loss.

May your desires be pious; may all your pious desires be fulfilled.

Take care.

Amit

* Suggested practice: Today, I will see obstacles as necessary to finding joy in success.
(For additional practices, visit Stressfree.org/Immerse/)

Week 8

During this week you'll cultivate a healthier attitude toward losses in life, and you'll feel connected with a world much larger than your family, workgroup, or neighborhood.

15. Gainful Losses

Overcoming the fear and regret of losing

Dear friend,

I fear losing. I fear loss of life, loved ones, respect, health, money, and much more. I know I am not alone in this fear. Research shows that for the same absolute change, the pain of loss feels twice as potent as the pleasure of gain. Understandably, we try our best to protect ourselves against losses.

For the losses already incurred, we simmer in regrets. Losing makes me sad and apathetic. Thinking of what ifs, could haves, and should haves, I start blaming others or myself. Unable to find peace in this blame game, the pain of loss multiplies and crowds my present moments.

I can't bypass losses. I also can't eliminate my fear of losing. However, I can soften my fears of a future loss—by thinking rationally about the probability of loss (instead of catastrophizing); taking actions to minimize the loss; thinking positively about the past, present, and future gains; and if all that doesn't work, imagining (and internally accepting) the worst-case scenario.

Five perspectives help decrease my regrets for a previous loss; the first three are more tangible, and the last two, more a matter of belief.

* First, I started my life with zero net worth, so everything I own today is a net gain.
* Second, every material possession, including my physical body, is finite. One day I will have to surrender it all. I can't control the timing of the surrender.
* Third, I should focus less on what I've lost and more on what I still have.
* Fourth, only the unneeded is taken away. I don't get to keep what I want; I only get to keep what I need.
* Fifth, this loss may be protecting me from some unknown loss or adversity that could have been much more sinister. So this loss might actually be an unrecognized gain.

When dealing with a substantial loss, I seldom succeed in applying these perspectives right away. After my initial grumbling, however, each of these insights provide me a useful mind-set to reevaluate the situation and rapidly recover my hope and energy.

The renewed hope and vitality help me explore and engage despite the fears, accept smaller losses more easily, look at the bigger losses with greater acceptance, and not discount what I didn't lose.

I have a choice. I can choose to wake up with fear, regrets, and self-doubt or with excitement about fulfilling a prosocial meaning. When I wake up with fear, I spend the day escaping that fear. When I wake up thrilled to fulfill a prosocial meaning, I spend my day immersed in activities that support that meaning. In order to choose meaning over fear, I need to develop a healthy attitude toward past and future losses.

May you find the strength to accept your losses and the foresight to minimize them.

Take care.

Amit

* Suggested practice: Today, I will focus more on what I have and less on what I have lost.
(For additional practices, visit Stressfree.org/Immerse/)

16. Family Tree

How big and connected is your family tree?

Dear friend,

Some of the biggest known family trees in the world—of Confucius, Lurie, and King Niall—make up a fraction of the real family tree of each one of us. The family tree of Confucius, for example, over eighty-six generations, is believed to have about three million descendants.

The actual size of your and my family tree (and also of Confucius's), if we could make all the connections, is much bigger. It has 110 billion members—the number of humans estimated ever to have lived on our planet. We are all individual leaves on a single large tree.

In fact, we are even more connected than that. The water in my body, which makes two-thirds of my weight, is connected to every body of water in the world. The air I breathe has touched countless people and trees. The energy that powers my conscious moments connects me to the sun. The life spark within me, I believe, is connected to every other life form.

When I help others, I help myself. The belief that I am a small strand in this big meshwork—that is, the world—makes me humble, fair, ethical, and well meaning. My mind, however, has a habit of forgetting. Without a recent reminder, I forget my pure intentions. I get busy with ordinary wants.

I need repeated reminders until my mind transcends its own limits and the limit set by my senses. Such a mind sees the universal design behind each eye, the shared vibration within each heartbeat—every heart sounds the same beat and beats the same tune. Loving the world is loving this universality while honoring its uniqueness.

May you feel connected to your true family tree, which extends to the farthest corners of the world; may this connection remove moments of loneliness from your life.

Take care.

Amit

*   Suggested practice: Today, I will treat friends as family, and family as friends.
(For additional practices, visit Stressfree.org/Immerse/)

Week 9

*D*uring this week you'll change your past by looking at it with a different lens and develop greater equanimity toward life's imperfections.

17. Past Can Be Changed

Have you lived well?

Dear friend,

I was born with a biological instruction manual that is stored in the six-foot-long DNA, tightly packaged in the nucleus of my microscopic cells. Most of the pages in this manual explain survival and safety procedures. Now that I have lived for nearly five decades, my thoughts and experiences have edited this manual and created a second version—one tweaked to provide greater peace and happiness without jeopardizing survival or safety.

I wish I had had this revised version several decades ago. I wish I could relive my past using some of the skills I now have learned. I can't. I do, however, have a choice.

I can look at yesterday differently than I did when I was experiencing it. I can be grateful for what was right, find right in what seemed wrong, and be compassionate for the suffering I and others endured. I can choose to accept my own and others' imperfections and forgive the hurts. I can try to find meaning in the pain that I endured. This new approach will help me live each day with purpose. It will help me be happier.

Past can be changed, by looking at it with a different lens. While everything could have been better than it was, if I am convinced that I now have the knowledge and skills to live a good future, then perhaps I have lived a good past.

May your hope and excitement for the future more than offset your regrets and hurts for the past.

Take care.

Amit

* Suggested practice: Today, I will live my day free of any regrets. (For additional practices, visit Stressfree.org/Immerse/)

18. Root and Fruit

A tree has to endure being a root for it to flower and fruit.

Dear friend,

When a seed germinates by absorbing water and nutrients, the first thing to emerge beneath the ground is the embryonic root, also called the radicle. Next the shoot appears and slowly threads its way above the ground. Leaves then materialize, by which time the sapling is established in its new home.

Most roots spend their time in damp filth and darkness. Roots, however, are the most essential part of a tree. They anchor the tree to the ground, transport water and nutrients, and store food. Every tree seeks flowers that lead to fruits (and seeds). Flowers wouldn't be possible, however, if the tree didn't have roots. The discomfort of the roots is the price the tree has to pay for the gift of the flowers.

The tree has a choice—either suppress its "root consciousness" or integrate that reality in its life. I like the latter option. It honors the struggles roots face each day.

My feet in the dirt help me learn the lessons I need in order to develop the requisite humility. The dirt experience nourishes me and teaches me how I might help others so they don't spend their lives focusing on the dirt. Just as a tree can't be alive without its roots, my life's difficulties nourish me in ways I can't fathom.

My experiences include both—damp dirt and boundless bliss. I should honor and integrate both the experiences and find meaning in them, so I can live a fuller and more useful life.

May your struggles be few; may each of your struggles make you stronger.

Take care.

Amit

*   Suggested practice: Today, I will see a difficulty as a good test of my resilience.
(For additional practices, visit Stressfree.org/Immerse/)

Week 10

During this week you'll practice being more intentional about how and what you think, and you'll wake up to discover a world more interesting and friendlier than you thought.

19. Thinking about Thoughts

Think intentional thoughts.

Dear friend,

Your calm face and still body belie a very active inner physical environment. As you read these words, perhaps you're totally unaware of your heart beating, diaphragm moving, lungs inflating, blood circulating, and intestines gurgling. In my medical training, I was amazed when I first heard the orchestra playing inside the human body—the heart beats, lung sounds, intestinal peristalsis, blood flow—brought to life by a simple stethoscope. Our inner orchestra is fairly loud—an unborn baby hears seventy to eighty decibels inside the womb (it's about as loud as the sound of a vacuum cleaner).

A calm face belies another inner noise, one that originates in thinking. By one estimate, each day, an average person thinks fifty thousand spontaneous thoughts. Our spontaneous thinking is chaotic and mostly repetitive from one day to the next. Each unit of thought has a context, but just like the random movement of the particles in a space (which scientists call the Brownian motion), tracked over a period of time, these thoughts go nowhere and don't accomplish much. Such excessive thinking produces inner congestion that stands in the way of our ability to connect with the world. Buried in our inner environment, we grow distant from the people closest to us and become strangers in our own homes.

Perhaps, just as a living heart beats, a living mind thinks. My automatic thoughts are a reflection of my mind's life. I shouldn't take their content and variations too seriously.

I believe the chaotic mind wanderings are a recent phenomenon. Not too far back in time, the human mind didn't have the luxury of mindless wandering, busy as it was protecting the self from the elements. Each technological progression that has made us safer and more comfortable has also freed up our attention, allowing us to think. This is an enormous opportunity for our species, and no other life form has access to it.

We need to make only one change to harness this opportunity—develop intentional thoughts. We should recognize the trivial nature of the vast majority of our spontaneous thoughts and instead choose to think intentional thoughts, ones that serve our conscience. Further, we should tether our intentional thoughts to timeless values of gratitude, compassion, acceptance, higher meaning, and forgiveness.

Thoughts aligned with these values are enormously precious. A substantial number of us thinking such thoughts would justify the tremendous effort nature invests each day to make human life possible. If, however, we were to spend our entire lives letting our minds think mostly repetitive, disorganized thoughts, we would be participating in a colossal waste of time and thought force—a tremendous lost opportunity. That would be sad.

May you think fewer thoughts, and may they be deep, happy, and kind.

Take care.

Amit

* Suggested practice: Today, I will think thoughts I am proud to own. (For additional practices, visit Stressfree.org/Immerse/)

20. Novel and Familiar

Find novelty in the familiar and familiarity in the novel.

Dear friend,

Most experiences fit on a continuum that ranges from predictable and familiar (which can be comforting but boring) to novel and unique (which is often fun and exciting but can be anxiety provoking). The same experience (e.g., a new neighbor) moves from novel to familiar as we learn and accommodate. We need both—familiar and novel—to fully experience life.

Novelty entertains the brain, and the brain, with its tendency to get easily bored when left alone, loves to be entertained. Research shows most students get bored in their school classes every single day. Further, as we age, we switch from actively seeking novelty to becoming a passive receiver of novelty.

Boredom doesn't just lead to a drab life; it can affect learning and predispose one to binge eating, drug abuse, and gambling. Sprinkling excitement in daily life thus can help one not only add more fun but also avoid self-harm. Despite all its awesomeness, though, novelty feels good only when in balance; excessive novelty can be overwhelming. That balance is provided by predictability/familiarity.

Familiarity provides a much-needed context to process novelty. It provides stability. Familiarity can feel dull; the dull and mundane, however, are sometimes necessary for regrouping and rejuvenating.

We need an optimal mix of the novel and familiar to keep life both sane and interesting. One way to do so is to search for novelty within the familiar and familiarity within the novel. When you find novelty within the familiar, you find your loved ones and friends interesting; when you find familiarity within the novel, you aren't overwhelmed by new colleagues or new responsibilities. This balance might allow a healthy dose of calm and excitement in your life.

May you create fun and meaning-filled days by balancing the excitement of novelty with the comfort of familiarity.

Take care.

Amit

* Suggested practice: Today, I will assume everyone I meet is unique and precious.
(For additional practices, visit Stressfree.org/Immerse/)

Week 11

$\mathcal{D}$uring this week you'll increase your strength by aligning your days with the deepest meaning and serving the biggest number, and you'll practice receiving in giving.

21. Power from Values

Increase your power...tremendously.

Dear friend,

The mayor of a city has greater influence on the city's happenings than a citizen without office; a country's president has greater power than the mayor. Everything else being equal, the bigger the group you serve, the greater your power. If you primarily work for yourself, you have some power; if you work for planet earth, you might feel much more passionate and powerful.

You also draw power from the truth you are trying to protect. Your own biases are less powerful than scientific theories; timeless wisdom even more powerful than scientific theories. When you work to protect your personal biases, you have limited power; when you work to protect timeless wisdom, your power multiplies.

In the real world, you'll be working for a group, a company, or a system, mostly to protect its underlying mission. In your own heart, however, you could work for planet earth and uphold timeless virtues. This belief will provide you tremendous inner strength and help you excel in your pursuits. It will also provide a secure inner compass that can guide you to always do the right thing.

May you be strong; may your strength come from the people and values you serve.

Take care.

Amit

* Suggested practice: Today, I will live by this single rule—just do the right thing.
  (For additional practices, visit Stressfree.org/Immerse/)

22. Bee and Flower

Giving is receiving, and receiving is giving.

Dear friend,

When you notice a bee alighting on a flower and mindfully sipping its nectar, you might think it is the bee that is receiving help. That is only half the truth. According to some estimates, bees pollinate a third of the food we eat. The cost of our food would double if bees disappeared from the planet. So the exchange between the bee and the flower is symbiotic. Superficially, the bee gets its ingredients for making honey; at a more subtle level, the bee carries the pollen, helping the flower fulfill its life's purpose (by transforming into fruits and seeds).

Life's exchanges are similar. While you may feel as if you are always the flower for a swarming, hungry hive, when you look deeper, you will realize that the bees are helping you fulfill your life's purpose. Sometimes that purpose may not be self-evident. You'll have to dig deeper for it. Such digging is very beneficial; several research studies conclude that helping or thinking about helping others can provide great benefits to you.

Research shows that people who donate their time often start feeling that they have more time, just as people who donate to charity feel wealthier. Research also shows that when you help others, you improve your physical health, decrease your risk of depression, become happier, increase your likelihood of getting a better job, and even live longer. People who accept your help are truly the angels who are serving you.

In summary, you are helped when you give or receive help; you are helping when you give or receive help.

In each experience, every person is the bee as well as the flower. Life's every exchange that is powered by good intentions benefits every participant. The precise flow of energy, in terms of time or goods, doesn't matter.

If you can fully internalize this truth, you are in for a treat all your life. It's a beautiful way to live.

May you be grateful for the help you receive; may you be grateful for the help you give.

Take care.

Amit

*   Suggested practice: Today, I will be grateful for those whom I am able to help.
(For additional practices, visit Stressfree.org/Immerse/)

Week 12

*D*uring this week you'll meditate on and be inspired by the goodness within you and focus on the positive aspects of your life, using the strength of positivity to dilute and transcend the negativity.

23. Self-Image

You are a good human being.

Dear friend,

My hats off to men and women who quit an addiction. It isn't easy to feel miserable, and resist what you know can relax you right away, amid a life full of stress, with a predisposed biology. Those who relapse after successful abstinence go through a well-understood process.

When the craving becomes irresistible, people convince themselves that puffing on a cigarette or two won't increase the world's suffering. Also, they think, "If I limit myself to just one or two, how bad can it be?" Such thinking often results in a full-blown relapse. In retrospect, one realizes that first puff started the cascade, yet in the moment, the puff seems benign and fully justifiable from within the person's perspective. When craving overwhelms a person, selfish preferences bleat like the voice of conscience.

Ignorance can't parse selfish preference from conscience. Ignorance (unlike conscience) generally focuses on the short term, supports a weaker action, and resolves a conflict by yielding and not exerting self-control.

Thinking, speaking, and acting from a place deep within us, through conscience, isn't easy. It takes courage and willpower. Such courage and willpower come from having a good self-image. The day you wake up convinced that you are a good human being; that a bad thought, word, or action is unbecoming of you; that you should model behavior that inspires others to live better lives—starting that day, you'll find the courage and willpower to live with conscience.

Surround yourself with people who accept you for who you are. Do not let the negatively biased ones trespass into your brain. If they do sneak in, do not let them stay for long. Minimize negative self-talk. Recognize that if you leave your mind on autopilot, it will default to self-critique. Don't let that happen. Keep this thought for the next hour—"I am a good human being; a bad thought, word, or action is unbecoming of me; I should model a behavior that inspires others to live a better life."

May you be valued and accepted for who you are, including by yourself.

Take care.

Amit

* Suggested practice: Today, I will not let anyone shake my firm conviction that I am a good person.
(For additional practices, visit Stressfree.org/Immerse/)

24. Pleasant vs. Unpleasant

Should unpleasantness dilute the pleasant or pleasantness dilute the unpleasant?

Dear friend,

I like watching sunrises and sunsets. Even though I know that the sun isn't actually setting, that the earth's movement causes the sunset, I can't help but see it as the sun moving down the horizon. The same is true regarding the illusion of pleasant and unpleasant. Even though I know that the biased prism of my mind (which habitually focuses on the short term and is limited by its evolutionary endowments) creates the certainty of pleasantness and unpleasantness, I can't help but see life's gains as pleasant and losses as unpleasant.

I also have a biased system that discounts the pleasant and inflates the unpleasant. This is the automatic me. I can't delete my innate software. But I can upgrade it.

I should recognize that pleasantness and unpleasantness are contextual and not absolute. A bright light that may feel pleasant on a cloudy day may be undesirable on a day you have a migraine headache. Research shows a sweater previously worn by a celebrity gives much greater pleasure than an identical new sweater. The same sweater once washed fails to give the extra pleasure. My perception of pleasure thus depends on a number of factors—the actual experience, its historical context, the rarity of the event, its dollar value, and more.

I should also recognize my innate negativity bias. I attend to, think about, trust, and remember negative information much more than positive information. I make negative opinions based on rumor or misinformation far faster than I make positive opinion based on facts. I get past the pleasant without savoring it. I inflate the unpleasant and dwell on it.

Awareness of this bias allows me to overcome my instinct of diluting the pleasant with the unpleasant. Instead, it empowers me to pick a new habit—diluting the unpleasant with the pleasant. It offers me a new lens to look at the world and provides me immediate access to a happier alternative.

I know that as I get older I will likely get better at noticing the positive and ignoring the negative (at least that's what the science says). I, however, don't have the patience to wait twenty more years. I wish to dilute my unpleasantness with the pleasant today. Becoming aware of my predispositions and my ability to choose is a good first step. I hope this knowledge inspires me to train my attention and mind-set so I can bring into this very moment the wisdom I might get when I am very old. I wish the same for you.

May the pleasant and good decorate your day and your mind.

Take care.

Amit

*   Suggested practice: Today, I will let only those things bother me that will continue to affect me in five years.
(For additional practices, visit Stressfree.org/Immerse/)

Week 13

During this week you'll contemplate on and practice different depths of gratitude, and you'll appreciate the simple and the ordinary, looking to discover a deeper meaning within them—the special and the extraordinary.

25. Five Depths of Gratitude

Can gratitude eliminate suffering?

Dear friend,

Gratitude comes with different depths. At one pole are people who don't know how to be grateful. They plunder the world, forever seeking more. They feel supremely entitled, and they harbor callous disregard for others' preferences.

A bit more awake are those who employ gratitude to thwart guilt. They use gratitude as a temporary escape into virtue so they don't feel so selfish in their hedonistic drive. Gratitude in them is an occasional companion, often contingent on something big and special happening, and generally doesn't translate into prosocial actions.

Next are people who are grateful for the small and simple. They are aware that what they receive is a collective effort of millions. Grateful thoughts visit their mind on most days and translate into occasional actions geared to help the world. They wish the whole world to be happy and are even willing to make a personal sacrifice for the benefit of others.

Further advanced are people who have gratitude as their constant companion. They are content. They have a very low threshold for happiness. Their personal needs are small, their thoughts predominantly prosocial. They still wish to acquire, but only so they can give more. Their gratitude doesn't lead to inaction; it actually plugs energy leakage.

Finally are people who are grateful even for adversities. They live in a state of surrender. Every experience to them is a meaningful gift. They have transcended the duality of good and bad. These are not dispassionate, apathetic people; quite the contrary, gratitude powers their passion and engagement. They wake up each day to create a more hopeful, happier, and kinder world.

The day the majority of the inhabitants of our world live in the constant company of gratitude, even amid adversity, will be the day we will have eliminated suffering.

May you feel grateful; may gratitude bring you lasting peace and happiness.

Take care.

Amit

*   Suggested practice: Today, I will stop before my meal and look at my plate with gratitude, thinking of the countless people who worked to make my meal happen.
(For additional practices, visit Stressfree.org/Immerse/)

26. Taste of Water

Water tastes better when you are thirsty.

Dear friend,

Scientists disagree on whether water has its own natural taste. Some believe that we have no taste buds for pure water. Like quiet is to the ears and dark to the eyes, water is null to the tongue—a base-line from which we can compare other tastes. Other scientists find unique brain areas activate when subjects drink water (particularly among rats) and believe that water has its own taste. Most agree that the taste of water depends on what is mixed in it and what you tasted just before (and is still sticking to your tongue).

Perhaps the taste of water is immaterial. The satisfaction and joy from drinking water depend less on its innate taste and more on how thirsty you are. On days you have wide access to water and drink liberally, it tastes bland and unappealing. But think about a day when you have been walking in the sun for an hour, sweating, with no access to water. Finally, when you get to a source of cool, pure water, won't it taste truly blissful, like the most satisfying drink ever?

The quality of your life's experiences depends on the nature of the experienced and the nature of your inner instrument (the experiencer). Between the two, the nature of the instrument is of much greater influence.

Once you recognize that each experience is unique and precious, each person is extra special, and you have finite moments to perceive them, you'll bring your complete presence and anticipation to savor your moments. An ordinary dinner will give the same joy as a multicourse gourmet meal prepared by a celebrity chef, your loved one's eyes will look better than sunrise in Hawaii, and connecting with an old acquaintance will feel like a twenty-five-year reunion. You'll awaken the child within you who knew how to have fun. You'll get more out of your days and your life. And water might taste better too!

May the music of joy fill every corner of your home; may your ears be attuned to hear that music.

Take care.

Amit

* Suggested practice: Today, when I eat a fruit, I'll remember the tremendous efforts nature took to create it.
(For additional practices, visit Stressfree.org/Immerse/)

Week 14

During this week, you'll find a path out of loneliness and practice being extra patient with others and yourself.

27. Good-Bye to Loneliness

Never allow yourself to feel lonely.

Dear friend,

Loneliness is a discrepancy between desired and perceived social connection. While solitude, which is a chosen state of isolation from social connection, can increase concentration, creativity, and productivity, the feeling of loneliness can inflict serious damage on physical and emotional health.

Infants whose biological needs are met but who are then left alone with no one to talk to don't survive. Children who aren't talked to develop depression, delinquency, and learning disabilities. Adults who feel lonely have a higher risk of depression, addiction, suicide, weight gain, hypertension, impaired immunity, heart attack, and stroke.

We are biologically designed to be nourished by connections. Just as hunger and thirst are protective albeit unpleasant feelings, the painful feeling of loneliness is a signal that alerts us to our physical and emotional vulnerability. Unfortunately, loneliness is widespread, with over 25 percent of people having no one in the world to confide in.

While loneliness is often related to a lack of meaningful people in one's life, more commonly, loneliness happens to those with many social connections. When our mind is locked alone inside, we feel vulnerable and unavailable for deeper connections. In this state we feel as if we are facing the load of the world alone. This loneliness affects at least someone in almost every single family. Our current societal structure, dependence on and obsession with technology, and work style all foster greater loneliness.

While you cannot always choose your physical proximity with others, you completely control your psychological proximity with others. Never allow yourself to be lonely. Be in physical or psychological presence of someone you admire or adore. Do not spend an inordinate amount of time inside your head with a wandering mind. Instead, think about people who make you happy, people you could be grateful for. Think about those who inspire you. Surround yourself with their pictures; listen to their voices.

All of this is worthwhile. The rewards are not only lower loneliness but also lower stress, greater happiness, better health, and more resilience.

May you always be in the company (physical or psychological) of someone you admire or adore.

Take care.

Amit

* Suggested practice: Today, I will take a ten-minute stroll in the mall and look at people, assuming they are all related to me. (For additional practices, visit Stressfree.org/Immerse/)

28. Little Something

You can always do a little something to lift someone's day.

Dear friend,

I am standing in front of a teller. I am a customer at this bank. But I am more than that. I am a father, husband, son, brother, cousin, friend, neighbor, colleague, professional, citizen, patient, seeker. I am protecting, in my mind, a world much larger than me. As I wait for the teller to help me, I jump from one identity to another.

I am in a hurry, and I expect quick, efficient service. The teller, however, seems busy, and in my judgment she could be more efficient.

I don't realize, however, that the teller also has all the identities and concerns I have, perhaps more.

She is tasked with serving fifteen to twenty customers every hour, a new customer every three to four minutes. She has run into all kinds of customers—difficult, ignorant, dishonest, entitled, and clumsy. Perhaps the customer prior to me gave her a tough time. She is expected to try her best to remain pleasant and professional to everyone who comes to her window. She also always has to be on alert—one wrong transaction could cost her a fortune.

That's not all. She could be struggling with an illness, concerned about her finances, sleep deprived, ill-treated, worried about her kids, or thinking about her parents. While she is helping her customers, she most certainly visits one of these places of hurt. If she didn't smile at me today, most likely it was because she was elsewhere at that moment. With so much going on in her life, she has the right to not smile, to be unhappy, even to be a little rude.

I should recognize her silent, invisible suffering. I should be patient even if she is slower than I wish her to be. Being patient is being kind. Patience connects me with her at a level deeper than it otherwise would be. I recognize her as a fellow human being, not as a means to an end. With a kinder presence, I feel good about myself.

Perhaps by being patient I can make her feel good about herself. That's all I can do. I can't ease her hurts or simplify her workload. I should certainly try not to make her life worse.

My visit to the bank uplifts me because I am able to exercise patience and preserve kindness. I am able to think and look deeper. What if I could do this all day long—to friends, colleagues, clients, loved ones, and myself? Each experience then would become uplifting. That would be nice.

May every person who connects with you today treat you with patience and grace; may you treat every person with patience and grace.

Take care.

Amit

* Suggested practice: Today, I will remember that no one can perform 100 percent all the time, including me.
(For additional practices, visit Stressfree.org/Immerse/)

Week 15

During this week you'll increase your depth of kindness and live with healthier optimism, believing that every suffering can, and eventually will, find healing.

29. Depths of Kindness

You can always be kinder.

Dear friend,

Research shows kindness activates anti-inflammatory genes in ourselves, while anger activates pro-inflammatory genes. You have a choice regarding which genes to activate today. Kindness also stimulates the brain's reward center. Kinder people are thus happier and healthier, and they live longer. Kind intentions that translate into kind actions are even more rewarding than kind intentions alone.

Kindness has both genetic and environmental bases. Scientists have found different genes associated with kindness. One of these genes is related to the oxytocin receptor (the bonding hormone). Further exploration of this gene has shown how it links with the environment to influence kind disposition—people with the kindness gene remain kind despite facing fear and difficulties; people without the kindness gene give up kindness quickly. Researchers estimate that about 30 to 60 percent of kindness is genetically determined, while the rest depends on life experiences and individual choices.

With this genetic and environmental interaction, people display different degrees of kindness. Some of us have a very negative view of life. We find it difficult to be kind to anyone.

Others plan kindness, as a way to get rewards. Their kindness is a conditional investment. They are kind to people of power, to those who can send goodies and toys their way. They are self-serving and see people as a means to an end.

Next are people who are kind to their supervisors as well as to those who depend on them. These are good people. They honor others. They are compassionate. They choose kindness, not because it will reward them, but because kindness is the right way to live. Kindness in humans generally reaches up to this depth. A deeper kindness than this isn't easy.

The next stage involves being kind to every part of creation, including even inanimate objects. People choosing such universal kindness respect creation and everything that is contained in it. Such kindness doesn't mean they'll start talking to their cutlery; it means they are gentle with everything they touch.

The final depth of kindness extends even to those who you know willfully and intentionally hurt you. It takes superhuman effort to continue to be kind to someone you know wants to hurt you. Precious few reach that depth. Such commitment to kindness anchors you in who you are, not what others push you into. It is a worthy goal to pursue.

Gauge your level of kindness and see if you can rise to the next level today.

May you look and think more deeply each day so you can access the well of kindness within yourself and others.

Take care.

Amit

* Suggested practice: Today, I will be extra kind to those who depend on me.
(For additional practices, visit Stressfree.org/Immerse/)

30. Healing

Did healing come before suffering?

Dear friend,

In the evolution of the universe, physics preceded chemistry, chemistry preceded biology, and biology—when it became complex enough to support insight, imagination, and intelligence through sculpting the human brain—spawned culture. Matter thus preceded life on our planet. Food came before hunger, air before breath, water before thirst. To expand this thought, I believe palliation came before pain, cure before disease, and healing before suffering.

Cure is often understood to mean the complete resolution of the illness, often with elimination of its underlying cause, indefinitely or for a very long time. Of the approximately seven thousand illnesses known to us, we have cures for only five hundred of them. For most others, cure is a potential not currently realized. We have to search for the cure and work hard to procure it. The cure otherwise remains an unrealized possibility. A cure reveals its secrets with a combination of effort, good intentions, and time. While we invest in science and expand our search so we can offer cures tomorrow, we have the ability today to offer a higher order of care—through healing.

Healing means restoring to wholeness, health, or original condition. Healing involves three domains—physical, psychological, and spiritual. In the physical domain, healing restores structure and function. In the psychological domain, healing restores hope, happiness, and fulfillment. Spiritual healing involves finding a deeper meaning for our suffering, and through that search, uncovering the meaning of life. Psychological and spiritual healing often entails letting go, and thus receiving clarity and insight through illness. Healing thus includes, and often transcends, the cure. Further, healing can happen without a cure or even a hope for one.

I can't eliminate my pain. But I can help postpone suffering, even when the mountain of pain seems taller than the clouds. I need my pain. If I lose pain sensitivity in my feet, I will lose my feet. If I became emotionally numb, I will lose the ability to empathize. Perhaps, the purpose of my pain is to make me aware of how something feels when it hurts, and through that awareness, become a more compassionate person.

My faith that healing was created before suffering starts my journey to overcome it. It gives me hope and energy to go out, make a difference, and, through that effort, find meaning.

May your every pain find its healing balm; may you help others find healing for their pain.

Take care.

Amit

* Suggested practice: Today, I will remember that what is right in my life outweighs what seems wrong.
  (For additional practices, visit Stressfree.org/Immerse/)

Week 16

*D*uring this week you'll find greater meaning and depth in each person you meet, and you'll be sensitive to the invisible suffering that surrounds most of us.

31. Boarding Pass

Lessons learned from a used boarding pass

Dear friend,

After a local flight, as I was about to toss a used boarding pass into the garbage, I took a second look at it. An hour prior, this was perhaps the most important document I had on me. It was the complete identification I needed to get on the airplane. I paid special attention to keep it secure. And now it had no value.

I opened the boarding pass and closely looked at the amazing zigzag of the bar code, which somehow made sense to a scanner and connected the pass to me. It didn't look like me at all, but it had my fingerprint. Each day, according to the latest statistics, a paper (or its electronic version) like this helps about eight million people travel across the globe. I thanked this little piece of paper for the value it served. And then I gently let it go.

I know that the meaning that connects me with many people, who are precious and indispensable in my life today, will fade. But people aren't boarding passes. My boarding pass, once used, literally lost its complete value at the termination of the flight. It couldn't serve anyone else. But people who move out of my life will become precious and indispensable to someone else. If I could be grateful to my used boarding pass today, I should be infinitely grateful to the people who came into my life and then moved into someone else's.

A few thousand years ago, an average tribe had about 150 members. Some researchers believe that 150 (often called Dunbar's number) is about the maximum number of meaningful social connections we can maintain, before life starts getting out of balance. Yet with agriculture, food processing, transportation, wholesale, retail, marketing, media, and food technology, hundreds of millions of people collaborate globally to bring my lunch plate. How can I not be grateful to each of them?

Irrespective of the current value to me, every person is precious and indispensable to someone. I should recognize that value and honor each person for who they are and what purpose they serve. I should also strive to find a connection in these unique individual purposes, for even though our flight destinations may seem different, once the journey is complete, the flights eventually will take us back to the same home.

The different purposes we all serve eventually unite to a single goal—to create a kinder, happier, and more hopeful world for our planet's children.

May you be privileged to create kindness, happiness, and hope for our planet's children.

Take care.

Amit

*   Suggested practice: Today, I will assume every person has infinite net worth.
     (For additional practices, visit Stressfree.org/Immerse/)

32. Invisible Suffering

What proportion of suffering is invisible?

Dear friend,

The planets, stars, and galaxies we can see today make up only 4 to 5 percent of the universe. We cannot see the rest, often called dark matter (27 percent) and dark energy (68 percent). Perhaps with more-refined instruments we will have better luck seeing the totality of the universe in the future.

Our brains, despite being as awesome as they are, are also very limited instruments. My brain can't sense any of the Wi-Fi networks that surround me, nor can it perceive the thousands of TV channels that my television receiver easily gains access to. More is unknown than is known to me.

The same is true for suffering. The greatest barrier to compassion isn't the absence of it; it is the limitation of compassion to a select few who we believe deserve it. With that attitude, you're likely to disregard the bulk of the suffering in the world—since it's invisible.

We see suffering in the hospital rooms, slums, famine-stricken lands, rejection letters, funerals, and courtrooms. With an average of two deaths every second on our planet (about sixty million in a year, more than 10 percent of which happen in children less than five), you can guarantee that, right at this moment, tens of thousands of people are mourning a loved one. (It isn't all gloomy though. Four babies are born every second; for each family in mourning, two are celebrating.)

The invisible suffering is everywhere. People endure it—in silence—while driving, showering, sleeping, eating, meeting, arguing, even partying. It starts the moment we wake up, accompanies us through the day, and often continues in sleep. We make valiant efforts to hide it—behind our smiling lips. But it's difficult to fool our own minds. Deep within us is a silent counter that logs our experience of suffering and slowly hollows our brain.

Our invisible suffering arises from feeling unworthy, powerless, hopeless, and lonely. The feeling that we lack control and our life doesn't have much meaning also causes suffering. Our tendency to compare and our vivid imaginations with a negative bias compound the suffering.

Despite all its negatives, however, of late I'm realizing that my invisible suffering has tremendous value. It has opened me up to the challenges of being human. It has made me more compassionate. It has inspired me to accept, find meaning, be more resilient, and become a better human being.

In the current world, most of us need personal experience with suffering to recognize suffering in others. We must transform into beings who are spontaneously compassionate so we won't need to suffer to become sensitive to suffering in others. I believe it is then that the meaning in suffering, visible or invisible, will vanish, and we will cease to suffer.

May courage and fortitude not leave your company through life's narrow lanes.

Take care.

Amit

*   Suggested practice: Today, I will be sensitive to the quiet struggles that most experience.
(For additional practices, visit Stressfree.org/Immerse/)

Week 17

*D*uring this week you'll experience more moments when you are fully present, and you'll help others, particularly children, discover a gentler and happier world.

33. Morning Drive

You have a choice.

Dear friend,

As I am driving to work in the morning, I see a school bus, with its red lights flashing, standing close to my cul-de-sac. I take a deep sigh; I am losing a precious minute here. My mind ruminates over the upcoming deadlines, things not done, the little imperfections.

The bus clears, and I cross the intersection. A quarter mile ahead, I see a traffic light that is presently green. I hate waiting at red lights.

I accelerate; my heart beats a little faster. I did it! I crossed just as the light turned orange. I saved another minute, but I did not quite like the transient palpitation.

A few seconds after entering the highway, I spy that my lane has three cars ahead of me while the other lane has only two. I shift my lane. Soon, however, I realize that the three cars in my original lane took the exit; the lane is now completely empty. A determined mini-van is accelerating from behind to claim the front-runner position. But I am a seasoned player, and within a blink, I surge ahead of the minivan. Somebody is unhappy, but that isn't me for now.

This pattern of jumping the orange lights, constantly perfecting the lanes, and beating the competition continues until I arrive at work. Bravo, I saved 180 seconds. What a great start to my day!

What did I lose? During the time I was in the car, I was literally fighting—with myself, traffic lights, other drivers, and time. I was increasing the risk of road rage and even an accident. (Each day in the United States, we lose about one hundred people, mostly young, from road-traffic accidents.)

In the one-minute halt at the cul-de-sac near my home, while watching the school bus, I could have admired innocent little kids getting into the bus, waved a warm hello to the bus driver, or even paused to think about why the school buses are yellow (buses began using this color in 1939 because it provides the best contrast to the black lettering before the sunrise in early morning). If the red light had stopped me, I could have enjoyed watching, from above the bridge, the traffic going both ways, like a colony of worker ants. I took the adrenaline shot and didn't enjoy it. It was much worse than drinking a tall latte; that at least soothes my taste buds.

The seasons have changed, and I have missed the fall colors. I have missed the wonderful hues that the sun daily paints on the clouds. I have even missed that many stores along my drive have redesigned their storefronts, and several new ones have come up.

Clearly, there is an alternative way to pay attention. If I am more present and focus more on enjoying the drive rather than saving every possible minute, I might add extra refreshing, nourishing time during the day for years to come, prevent possible mishaps, and become a more courteous driver. I do have a choice. We all do.

May you remember that you always have a choice, the choice to be fully present.

Take care.

Amit

* Suggested practice: Today, I will take out an old photo album and look at my loved ones' older pictures.
(For additional practices, visit Stressfree.org/Immerse/)

34. What Should Children Crave?

A healthy craving

Dear friend,

Little children experience the greatest joy and the greatest suffering. Children have fewer worries, unaware as they are of the countless daily threats you and I can learn about by clicking a few links on the Internet or spending a few minutes on any headline news. They seek excitement from the moment they start their day. They also have much less imagined suffering. The world is novel for them—there's so much to learn and explore. Their mind-wandering apparatus isn't fully mature yet. Hence, they suffer less.

But the same attributes impair their ability to process adversity. With their less mature brain and relative inexperience, they have a limited ability to problem solve. Because they cannot project too far, they exaggerate the imperfections of the present moment. They are surrounded by phenomenal attractions over which they have little control. They lack the sophistication to express their innocence and often are disciplined when they should be understood. I can't begin to imagine the suffering experienced by a three-year-old who gets a ten-minute time-out in a dark pantry for speaking out loud to an adult who could not understand the child's desire to turn the water faucet on by him- or herself.

None of this is helped by the fact that the grown-ups who surround the children have all the power, all the access to resources, and five times their size. Some adults are unpredictable and unkind. For all of these reasons, children suffer.

The greatest threat to a child's happiness is company of an adult or adults who aren't kind to them. Research shows that the single most important variable in the resiliency among children is the company of an adult who loves them and knows how to show it. That adult doesn't always have to be a parent—it can be a neighbor, friend's parent, teacher, counselor, pastor, or anyone else who comes in contact with the child.

I believe the single most important thing we can do to compensate for our children's neural limitations is to get them habituated to kindness. Let them grow in a world where kindness is the norm. Let them crave kindness. Raised voices and temper should surprise them. Children raised with kindness will emanate kindness. They will find kind partners. They will be healthier, more successful, and happier, and they will create a kind world. By being kind to the child next to you, you are truly paying it forward.

May every little one in your family be surrounded by a garland of love.

Take care.

Amit

*   Suggested practice: Today, I will be extra patient with children, remembering that they often can't think of the long term.
    (For additional practices, visit Stressfree.org/Immerse/)

Week 18

*D*uring this week you'll commit to forgiveness by finding greater meaning in it, and you'll be careful about who enters your thoughts.

35. The Best Revenge

The best revenge is forgiveness.

Dear friend,

Forgiving those who attacked them or their tribe, stole cattle, and burned their homes would have made no sense to hunter-gatherers, who commonly died from external injuries, accidental or intentional. During those times, they would have construed forgiveness as a sign of weakness. They would have naturally responded by planning revenge, which would have provided some solace. Because we have inherited their predispositions, it is no wonder that contemplating revenge activates our brain's reward areas.

Times have changed. Forgiveness makes much more sense now, for at least two reasons. First, revenge and its associated anger are seldom protective in modern times, because most modern hurts (but not all) are symbolic and psychological. Think about the last five times you cried. Was it because of physical pain or emotional pain? More likely, emotional pain, isn't it? Second, our greatest mortality risk now comes from cardiovascular disease and cancer (and not injuries). Bottled-up anger and its associated stress predispose us to both of these, and several other common causes of death. While lack of forgiveness helped us survive in the treacherous past, in modern times, forgiveness aids survival.

Psychological and emotional damage hurts you at an additional, deeper level. Others hurt you by affecting your world view. They hurt you by taking away your hope, faith, optimism, and belief in the goodness of humanity. They steal your innocence. Don't let anyone do that to you.

In response to a hurt, you can plan either worldly revenge or emotional and spiritual revenge. When you exact a worldly revenge, by hurting people back, your mind may feel transiently uplifted, but deep within, you don't win.

When you forgive, you frustrate others in their efforts. You stop them in their tracks. You don't allow them to increase your risk of heart attack, stroke, cancer, or dementia. On the contrary, you grow as a result of their efforts to stop you. That indeed might be the perfect revenge.

May the world not send you pain; may your pain heal with forgiveness.

Take care.

Amit

* Suggested practice: Today, I will forgive my own past mistakes and accept myself as I am.
  (For additional practices, visit Stressfree.org/Immerse/)

36. Who Lives in Your Brain?

People who live in your brain change it.

Dear friend,

In my home I invite the kind people, the people I enjoy and consider my friends. In my thoughts, however, I invite the unkind people more often—the people who hurt me, judged me, or made me feel small. Further, the unfriendly and unkind people stick in my head much longer.

Each person who visits my brain carves a unique space. Under the direction of the hippocampus, a seahorse-shaped structure in the inner part of the brain, my brain stores memories across its multitude of networks. Memories that are of immediate survival value, physical or emotional, are deeply integrated and more easily accessible. I can't forget people who hurt me in the past or could hurt me in the future. Memories of past injuries and concerns about future injuries hurt my present.

When my brain hosts unkind people, it suffers damage at their hands. Initially, the damage is subtle, and it goes unnoticed. But over a period of time, the microinjuries deplete my life of vitality and predispose me to anxiety, depression, and variety of chronic medical conditions. Such cumulative damage degenerates my brain, predisposing it to dementia. (Research shows that excessive cortisol and related chemicals, which are released by chronic stress, cause loss of neurons in the brain.)

My brain's penchant to spend an inordinate amount of time with unkind people is its default setting. I need to choose otherwise. I need to remember that when my brain hosts kind people, it feels secure, worthy, and loved. Kind people help me build a stronger brain. (Research shows that feeling nurtured and loved releases endorphins, oxytocin, and growth factors such as BDNF, which cause neuronal growth in the brain.)

Since I can choose my thoughts, I can choose whom to invite and give residence in my brain. I just need to remember and exercise that choice.

May you not need to visit the hurt-filled corners of your brain today; instead, may you frequent the brain's rest areas, resorts, and sacred places.

Take care.

Amit

* Suggested practice: Today, I will remember at least five people who helped me in the past.
(For additional practices, visit Stressfree.org/Immerse/)

Week 19

*D*uring this week you'll convert your personal gifts into blessings for others and choose to focus on what is right in the other person rather than what is wrong.

37. Gratitude Empowers Compassion

What is the perfect way to repay for your gratitude?

Dear friend,

As I write these words and you read them, someone on our planet is very thirsty with no water in sight, someone is very hungry with no access to food, someone is lonely with no hope for a kind word, and someone is being physically harmed with no one to help.

I hope no hurt, physical or emotional, unintentional or intentional, ever goes unattended. But that hope is unlikely to be met in my lifetime. We have eradicated smallpox, but we haven't eradicated child abuse. We have prolonged survival for many chronic diseases, but the depression rates globally continue to increase. We keep getting wealthier but not happier. Overall, we have done a great job of improving the physical world but have lagged miserably with influencing the emotional world. Clearly we have a lot of work to do.

If at this moment I am not experiencing physical or emotional torment (as many of my countless fellow beings are), I have a responsibility. I have a responsibility to be grateful; to think, speak, and do good; and to feel compassion toward those who are suffering. If I don't think gratitude and feel compassion, then not only am I missing out on life, but I am not fulfilling my responsibility, and I am not being just to those who are suffering.

If I have an opportunity today to be grateful, then I have a responsibility to be compassionate. The things that I am grateful for boost my energy, which I should use to power my compassionate thoughts, words, and actions. We don't need stellar new technologies to create a happier world. We need to harness the power of gratitude and compassion.

May you be more grateful and compassionate; may you recognize that it's truly a privilege to be grateful and compassionate.

Take care.

Amit

* Suggested practice: Today, I will think less about my own struggles and instead remember that everyone around me has many struggles, often worse than mine.
(For additional practices, visit Stressfree.org/Immerse/)

38. Z Check

You have a choice in what you focus on.

Dear friend,

I was talking to an air force fighter pilot about the importance of prioritization and focus. Halfway into our discussion, he shared how he lands his aircraft. He would do what they call a Z check, to scan all the cockpit gauges and indicators. This Z check almost always indicates that one or two gauges are off. At that moment he has to prioritize—should he focus on landing the plane or think about why that needle is off? He is trained to recognize danger. He is also trained to disregard minor malfunctions. With this dual set of skills, he has landed the plane safely each time.

He correlated the way he lands his plane with our discussion about life. Curiously, he hadn't applied his air force lessons to the rest of his life. As a result, he wasn't piloting his family life well. He was reactive toward his wife, focusing on the minor imperfections. Even at cruising altitude at home, when things were outwardly quiet, he was busy with memories of hurts and regrets. Worse, he had a tendency to launch preemptive missiles to avert future disagreements. Some of these disagreements were totally imaginary with low potential of materializing. His personal life was thus dissatisfying.

At the end of our discussion, he left with the thought that if only he lived his life with the same gentleness and care with which he flew and landed his plane, he would be much happier.

Choose to reevaluate something trivial about your loved one that has bothered you of late. Let go of it today and instead focus on something profound that is right about him or her. Your moments of togetherness are finite and fewer than you think. Make the most of each of them.

May you be surrounded by good people; may you focus on their goodness rather than their inadequacies.

Take care.

Amit

* Suggested practice: Today, I will accept one imperfection in my loved one, because I am grateful for all that is right about him or her. (For additional practices, visit Stressfree.org/Immerse/)

Week 20

During this week, you'll recognize and harness the power in your thoughts, and you will try your best to forgive the past, knowing that revenge only breeds counter revenge.

39. Subtle and Gross

Do thoughts create the brain?

Dear friend,

My thoughts host my desires. Desires prompt seeking, which leads to actions. Actions transform matter into its more complex forms. That's how the world changes itself. Our thoughts are thus very powerful, for they have created the present world, and will shape the future world. No wonder, across the generations, several authors and philosophers have scribed this basic idea—the pen and the word are mightier than the sword.

Within my physical body, my thoughts are hosted by my brain. Each thought is my brain working out a particular network. The greater workout a network experiences, the more real estate it acquires—a phenomenon scientists call neuroplasticity. The changing real estate reorganizes the human brain.

When you start playing piano or violin, you thicken the areas of your brain that help with control and coordination of the hand movements, and also strengthen attention, memory, planning, and inhibitory control. When you start driving taxis (without the GPS), you thicken the part of the brain that helps you remember directions (posterior hippocampus); when you learn to think more rationally, your brain's networks involved in problem-solving, cognitive control, and emotional regulation (different parts of the prefrontal cortex) become more active. The structure of your brain tomorrow thus depends on your current choices and the quality and content of your thoughts.

The subtle organizes and transforms the gross. The gross might seem like it hosts the subtle, but it is the subtle that connects the nodes of the gross. The best way I can make my gross beautiful is by making my subtle beautiful, which translates to thinking good and wholesome thoughts.

May you create a beautiful brain tomorrow by thinking fewer, kinder, and happier thoughts today.

Take care.

Amit

* Suggested practice: Today, I will choose to think like someone whom I truly admire.
(For additional practices, visit Stressfree.org/Immerse/)

40. Settling Scores

Can scores ever be settled?

Dear friend,

I wish I never needed to seek forgiveness or forgive anyone. But my vulnerabilities are many and my desires protean. My seeking gets frustrated at times, by others or by pure chance, creating moments I wish I could forget and forgive.

Forgiveness, however, doesn't come naturally to me. When I try to forgive, I feel I am being unfair to myself. I feel I am enabling the other person, that I risk being seen as weak, predisposing myself to future hurts. All of this pushes forgiveness away.

The alternative to forgiveness is seeking revenge. The idea of revenge offers a transient refuge to the human mind. Revenge promises to prevent future attacks and restore justice. Thinking and planning revenge is pleasurable, for it activates the brain's reward center. Research shows the greater the activation of the brain's reward center, the harsher the planned revenge.

Research also shows that revenge originates in the belief that hurting others will comfort the avenger. This belief, however, doesn't translate into lived experience. When you hurt others in revenge, you increase your ruminations about the event (trying to feel justified for your action) and thus actually feel worse. Further, revenge seldom feels fair—the avenger feels that the offender got away with little punishment; the offender feels the revenge was disproportionate to the offense.

My daily lived experience matches with scientific findings. When I have been a recipient of retribution, I have always found it unjust and disproportionate to the hurt I caused. I have seldom connected my own indiscretion with the revenge I received. Each settled score thus creates a new unsettled score.

If I wish to end this toxic back and forth, I need to embrace forgiveness. There is no other recourse. I should recognize my instinct of revenge, delay acting upon it, understand the full perspective, try to validate the other person to the extent I can, try to accept to the extent I can, and give forgiveness a chance.

Minds that marinate in revenge can't create a happy, kind, sustainable world. A world filled with thoughts of revenge is a world filled with horrors. Revenge isn't always benign, as when bad-mouthing someone or not replying to an e-mail. Sinister revenge can range from sending a computer virus to damaging someone's career or opening fire on the innocent.

I wish to live my life where I started—free of any thoughts of hurt or desires for retribution. I wish to end my life where I started—with no one I need to forgive. I must remember what Confucius said: "Before you embark on a journey of revenge, dig two graves."

May your day start with the score of love-all; when your day ends, may the score still be love-all.

Take care.

Amit

* Suggested practice: Today, I will forgive in gratitude for the many times I have been forgiven.
(For additional practices, visit Stressfree.org/Immerse/)

Week 21

*D*uring this week you'll be grateful for those who help you become a better person by informing you about your imperfections, and you will create synchrony among your thoughts, words, and actions.

41. Mistake Doctor

Those who point out your mistakes are your well-wishers.

Dear friend,

As a physician I completely believe in prevention. Breast cancer treated at stage 1 has almost no negative effect on survival, while 80 percent of the patients diagnosed at stage 4 do not make it past five years. Diagnosing and curing cancer early in its course prevents children from losing their mom or dad, protects a loving son or daughter, prevents toxic side effects of treatment, and does so much more. Most patients are grateful when a physician detects their cancer early. I too will be, if that is my experience.

Not so for my mistakes. I feel angry when I am told I am wrong—about a thought, word, or action. I fiercely defend my version of the truth. When someone rejects my truth, I feel that person is rejecting my entire being. I seldom recall being truly grateful to anyone who helped me by showing me how I was incorrect.

There are many reasons. Perhaps I can't take rejection, have an inflated or insecure sense of self, am uncomfortable accepting I could be wrong, get insulted easily, feel like I am being intentionally demoralized when shown a different viewpoint, etc. Barring a few exceptions, none of this is helpful.

I should consider my mistakes as early cancer. Someone helping correct my errors—particularly a loved one, friend, or colleague who cares about me—is like a doctor detecting an early cancer. If I can be truly grateful to the doctor who saved my life by diagnosing my cancer early, I should be equally grateful to the person who helped remove the potential cancers lodged in my mind. Humility will help me develop such a mature attitude.

Cultivating humility can teach me the path to learning from feedback. Humility doesn't mean I lower myself compared to others. True humility helps me nurture a healthy self-worth, reminds me we are all equally worthy, helps me avoid comparing myself to or judging others, and guides me to be open and willing to learn. I wish myself the gift of humility so instead of snapping, I can bend in the storm, and thus save much grief for many.

May you be surrounded by caring people who can critique you; may you be humble and graceful in receiving critique.

Take care.

Amit

*   Suggested practice: Today, I will be grateful to those who let me know how I am wrong.
(For additional practices, visit Stressfree.org/Immerse/)

42. Three Selves

Integrate your multiple identities.

Dear friend,

I am *Homo sapiens*. Like most fellow beings of my species, I have forty-six chromosomes in my cells. I think; I breathe; I can't fly, but I can walk, run, and swim. I have many identities based on my relationships, race, country of origin, gender, intimacy preference, profession, neighborhood, generation, personality type, food preference, and more. Many of these identities are well defined. No one can argue about my species, gender, country of origin, or generation. But some identities are a matter of individual opinion (or bias).

Based on how you see me, you could consider me selfish or altruistic, gentle or rough, soft spoken or brash, likable or annoying, boring or interesting, and so on. In fact, based on these "soft characteristics," I exist in at least three versions. One is what I think of myself. Another is what others think of me. And the third is who I really am. These three versions aren't mirror images.

The less I am self-aware and the greater I pretend, the more separation exists between the three versions of me. I believe my life would be simplest if the three versions were very similar—ideally identical. How do I go about bringing this integration? I have a three-step plan.

First, I should sketch an idealized version of me. This would be the version I want to read about in my eulogy. This would be the version that I am proud to read about to my grandkids.

Second, I should start thinking and living like my idealized version. I should think thoughts I am proud to own, and align my words and actions with those thoughts. I should commit my life to kindness. With effort, I hope I will eventually reach a point where my thoughts, words, and actions will be in harmony. At that point, my self-perception and my actual self will integrate. I will have only two versions left—what others think of me and who I am.

The third step depends on others. I hope that as I cultivate consistent kindness, others will start to recognize it. Eventually, if I am lucky, they will see me as I am. Then the real me and others' perceptions of me will be identical. I will be in complete harmony with myself.

The integration has to start with me—I must conceptualize my idealized self and align my thoughts, words, and actions with that self. I believe, once I reach that point, I will become a much more effective instrument to help others find peace and happiness and integrate their three versions.

May you live in a world that welcomes virtuous thoughts, true words, and kind actions; may you help create such a world.

Take care.

Amit

*   Suggested practice: Today, I will think about how I wish to be remembered.

(For additional practices, visit Stressfree.org/Immerse/)

Week 22

During this week you'll be more intentional about filling your moments with healing thoughts and perspectives, and you'll wisely decide which problems and projects to engage with and which to let go.

43. Does Time Heal?

Time is the stage on which healing is enacted.

Dear friend,

Different philosophers, physicists, and religious authorities have different perspectives on the nature of time. Most of us see the past as the past, while some tribes look at the past as the future (and the future as the past). Some track the movement of the sun, while others track the moon. Some see time as linear and others as circular. Some see time as finite, others as infinite. Some consider it real and others as unreal.

Countless instruments have been designed to measure time—T squares, sundials, water clocks, hourglasses, pendulums, clocks and watches of various types powered by gravity, springs, electricity, and now atomic clocks that are accurate to within seconds over millions of years. Each of these instruments measures time in its basic unit— seconds. One second is a large unit with respect to the speed of light or oscillation frequency of the cesium atom. For us at the conscious level, seconds thread together to create minutes, hours, and days. It is at this level that life expresses itself.

The drama of life is hosted by two stages—the gross stage of the world and the subtle stage of the time. Time provides the scaffold for life to weave its tapestry. Time, however, has been credited with more than it can deliver. Time is a passive witness that doesn't interfere with life. Instead, time lets life play on it, just as a piano lets anyone with fingers play on it. Time doesn't heal or hurt; time just allows the dominant perspective to express itself.

Time can comfort or create hurt. Time can comfort your hurts by creating a distance from the pain of losses and adversity. Distance, however, only takes the edge off; in order to heal, the mind has to find different and more adaptive ways of looking at the experience and fill the void with moments that compensate for the hurt with hope and positivity.

Time can deepen the pain by letting the mind create additional perspectives around misunderstandings and pick more hurts, forming a large beehive out of a minor initial slur. Our expectations have also changed over the generations. In the ancient past, if you and I met and walked away without punching each other's noses, it was a good encounter. Not so now. Now, even minor disagreements or disapprovals, such as a little feeling of being disrespected, are enough to reject people outright. We have become very sensitive, and we easily get offended.

Such sensitivities hurt relationships. If you aren't secure in relationships, you'll struggle with building the nest where little ones can thrive. That's not a recipe for a healthy society.

If you wish to find healing, you'll have to let go of the need to always be approved and deemed right. You'll have to lower your expectations and focus on how you can help rather than be helped. And when a crack appears, you'll have to seal it as soon as possible, long before it deepens into a Grand Canyon.

Time can heal or multiply suffering. The outcome depends on what you fill the time with. Time filled with hurts and slurs worsens suffering; time filled with wisdom and love heals suffering. Time is the stage on which healing happens. The healer for me is my own mind, helped by yours.

May you fill your time with healing perspectives born of wisdom and love.

Take care.

Amit

* Suggested practice: Today, I will assume an inconvenience is protecting me from a mishap that could have been much worse.
   (For additional practices, visit Stressfree.org/Immerse/)

44. Dropped Balls

Which balls should you let drop?

Dear friend,

Juggling, the art of tossing and catching objects while keeping them in perpetual motion, has been around for at least four thousand years. From a favored art to a disgraceful activity to a resurgence in the mid-twentieth century, juggling has become a popular sport, and most cities have a juggling club. We all can learn juggling, and with time and effort, even master it. However, no matter the intensity of training, there is an upper limit to the human ability to juggle. No juggler can keep thirty balls in the air. Despite all its awesomeness, our brain has finite capacity.

An average person these days has over 150 undone tasks at any time. Our brain carries a greater load of uncertainty than it was designed for. Given the finite number of minutes you have each day and the finite number of days left in your life, you'll have to prioritize. You'll have to make the tough choice of which balls to keep in the air and which to let drop.

I should recognize that not all the balls I have in the air are of equal merit. I should let a few tumble so I can pay better attention to the ones more personally meaningful. I should also recognize that some balls are more vulnerable than others. Perhaps they are made of glass; if they fall, they'll break. These balls contain relationships, particularly with people who feel vulnerable. I should avoid letting those balls drop.

I should also give myself respite from juggling, by finding moments during the day when I choose to exit the fast lane. Research shows that the human brain gets tired after about 90 to 120 minutes of continuous activity. After that time, error rates go up and efficiency goes down. Depending on the nature and intensity of your work (and your innate ability), you might get tired much sooner. If you wish to avoid errors and preserve your vitality, give yourself frequent rest.

In today's world, you can't help but be a juggler. But if you juggle fewer balls for shorter time, take extra care with the glass balls, and give yourself occasional respite so you can recharge, you'll be much more effective at running your life.

May you choose the option of making a not-to-do list, just as you make a to-do list.

Take care.

Amit

* Suggested practice: Today, I will recognize and accept that there are times I won't get the best deal.
  (For additional practices, visit Stressfree.org/Immerse/)

Week 23

During this week you'll recognize the extraordinary within the ordinary and find greater meaning in the daily little challenges.

45. Is Normal Phenomenal?

Recognize the extraordinary within the ordinary.

Dear friend,

It takes a full year for a baby's cooing sounds to turn into words, and another one to two years for these words to join into a simple conversation. Adult speech entails coordination of seventy to one hundred muscles, with more neurons needed to speak than are needed for a hundred-meter sprint.

Speaking, eating without spilling, walking, running, reading, writing, potty training—these are all phenomenal achievements that we celebrate when we raise a child. But when the child grows up, we forget what a big deal it was to watch him or her take the first step.

Then, for some of us, arrives a day when we lose one or more of these faculties. It could be from stroke, another medical condition, trauma, or something else. We become a child again and try to relearn. It is then that we are reminded of the true value of what we had. If we don't fully recover, we remember the good old days when we could speak, walk, eat, or laugh.

Let that not happen to you. Do not close your eyes to the ordinary that is miraculous. What seems ordinary is a product of a series of miracles. Normal is actually phenomenal.

If you don't see it that way, it is because you aren't aware of the complexity that makes the ordinary happen. The greatest miracle is your ability to think and speak the word *miracle* and be conscious while doing that. Wow!

May you celebrate the ordinary—finding the rare, the timeless, and the precious within the mundane.

Take care.

Amit

*   Suggested practice: Today, I will be thankful for the silent working of my many body systems.
(For additional practices, visit Stressfree.org/Immerse/)

46. Little Problems

❧

The gift of minor irritations

Dear friend,

Our home recently had an unwelcome visitor—a mouse. Let's call him Mr. Mousey. Mr. Mousey left his mark—his droppings—all over the dwelling, putting our entire family on alert. We went on a cleaning rampage, setting up traps to catch him before he could invade the pantry. We finally caught Mr. Mousey and escorted him out. During the two days he stayed at our home, we forgot that many parts of the world were still at war, communicable diseases were spreading, and floods were threatening a town.

Problems have a way of focusing the brain. The better defined the problem, the easier it is for us to focus. The most difficult problems, however, are often complex. The finiteness of all of us, the uncertainty of the future, countries at war, poverty, world hunger, our vulnerability to suffering—these are big, currently unsolvable problems. If a mind gets mired in these, it can't find an easy escape. Maybe our daily small problems, which keep us busy and are much better defined and more easily solved, are a good distraction. The small problems fill our very limited attention.

The human attention capacity is constrained by the processing ability of our conscious mind, estimated at 120 bits per second. One person talking to you takes up about 60 bits. Thus, you can barely listen to the demands of your child while planning the day with your partner. This might explain why grocery shopping with three young kids is unlikely to be a fun experience.

While this processing limit predisposes us to mental fatigue from the information overload we face (the world has already produced over 300 exabytes of data), it might serve us well by limiting our ability to process hurts. When we are buried in small problems, we don't have the bandwidth to think about bigger, less defined, relatively unsolvable problems.

The problem is the separation between the current perceived situation and the desired situation. Because we are vulnerable to mortality, that separation will exist, so we will forever be solving problems. A healthy mind-set toward problems might help.

I should look at little solvable problems as gifts—they prevent me from getting overwhelmed by bigger unsolvable problems. I should accept the bigger, poorly defined, relatively unsolvable problems even as we collectively try to address them. When viewed with a mature perspective, my problems, instead of remaining problems, might become stepping stones toward deeper meaning.

May the problems you face today be simple and solvable; may each problem steer you toward your life's deeper meaning.

Take care.

Amit

* Suggested practice: Today, I will consider solvable challenges as welcome distractions.
(For additional practices, visit Stressfree.org/Immerse/)

Week 24

During this week you'll actively nurture your sense of wonder and excitement and practice living your day with your core values.

47. Childlike

Preserve your innocence and curiosity.

Dear friend,

Kids are self-centered. They can't think abstractly. They often don't treat others the way they want to be treated. They lack patience. Yet they are the apples of our eyes. Our entire life revolves around them. They are infinitely precious. They define our life's purpose. What is it that makes them so special to us (beyond the genetic connection)? One attribute is their innocence.

Little children are free of blame. They lack awareness of evil. They don't quickly judge or improve others. They completely trust those who care for them. They move past their hurts very quickly. They don't spend their day scheming how to impress or dominate others. They are spontaneous and aren't embarrassed easily.

Innocence in children becomes wisdom in adults. When we become wise, we stop thinking about and pay less attention to evil. We don't quickly judge or seek to improve others. Believing everyone is trying to do their best, we trust others. We move past our hurts quickly. We don't spend our day scheming how to impress or dominate others. We are spontaneous, less self-conscious, and less likely to get embarrassed.

If you look at the above two paragraphs, you'll notice that I have highlighted the same gifts—attributing them to innocence in children and to wisdom in adults. Perhaps, then, wisdom means choosing to become innocent like a child, after learning the lessons life provides us.

This "acquired innocence" that comes from wisdom is resilient, and it can provide lasting happiness, unlike kids' happiness, which is vulnerable. Kids are only happy when treated well. They depend on the world to keep them happy. Their happiness and innocence is also coupled with ignorance and lack of responsibility. You can't trust a two-year old with even the littlest chore.

Thus you can't be a child. But you can awaken the child within you that has a sense of wonder and innocence. To me that is wisdom.

May your innocence be nurtured and valued as a treasured expression of your wisdom.

Take care.

Amit

* Suggested practice: Today, I will play one game I played as a child. (For additional practices, visit Stressfree.org/Immerse/)

48. Organized

How best to organize your day

Dear friend,

A day is 1,440 minutes. During a day, on an average, your heart beats one hundred thousand times, and you take twenty thousand breaths. No one precisely knows the number of thoughts per day. Estimates range from a few thousand to up to fifty thousand. In a typical day, you burn approximately two thousand calories, of which about four hundred (20 percent), are used by the brain. The brain spends a fraction of these calories on thinking. Let's say that's about a quarter of the calories consumed by the brain (one hundred calories). So a single one-hundred-calorie energy bar transforms itself into the brain activity that powers your entire thought force for the day.

The primary drivers of your thinking, and thus your speech and actions, are your intentions. Broadly, your day could be organized around three core themes—fun, chores, or wisdom.

For a preschooler, the day is organized around fun. They constantly seek novelty. Every object, little or big, is a potential toy. Every person is a potential playmate. Every activity is a part of the game.

Adults often organize the day around chores. The moment adults wake up, the first few thoughts concern what needs to be done and how they will do those things. Time in the shower, at the breakfast table, during the drive, in the office, during the drive back, with family in the evening—is most commonly spent thinking—about chores or relationships. There is, however, another way.

You can organize your day around wisdom and its derived principles. You can anchor your thoughts, words, and actions to one of the five principles—gratitude, compassion, acceptance, higher meaning, and forgiveness. Focusing on the principles doesn't mean you spend all your day chanting their names. It means they provide a background to how you experience the day.

As an adult with numerous responsibilities, I can no longer organize my day around fun. I also don't wish to organize my day around chores. I wish to tether my day to the principles. I believe if I can do that, I will be happier and more focused; I will have more fun, and perhaps I might even complete more chores.

May you transform your daily chores and boredom into moments lush with fun and meaning.

Take care.

Amit

*   Suggested practice: Today, I will think about the higher meaning I am fulfilling.
(For additional practices, visit Stressfree.org/Immerse/)

Week 25

During this week you'll practice being grateful for the little and larger blessings by finding positivity even within adversity, and you'll live your days aligned with your deepest meaning.

49. Rx Gratitude

How gratitude can help tide over the adversity

Dear friend,

That was a tough day. Our younger daughter, Sia, had a raging infection. Her fever was 105 degrees. She looked really unwell. We took her to the ER. After elaborate testing, we received the diagnosis, she was prescribed antibiotics, and we drove back home.

After a few minutes of sharing worries, we began counting our blessings. Her illness had been diagnosed in time; it was curable; we had access to medical care with kind, competent staff; the world has antibiotics now; her immune system is normal…

We had a whole lot to be grateful for. As we started compiling the list of what was right, our attention shifted. By the time we reached home, we felt good and secure. We were focusing on solutions and had quit struggling with all the what ifs.

Sia recovered quickly. We learned that even in the midst of a very difficult situation, our minds can find aspects to be grateful for. Further, such search can provide hope and comfort and stop unhelpful, energy-depleting ruminations and worries.

May the power of gratitude transform your memories of plight into moments of delight.

Take care.

Amit

*   Suggested practice: Today, I will not live in fear of failure or loss. (For additional practices, visit Stressfree.org/Immerse/)

50. Meaning, Personal and Global

It is easier and more useful to make your life more meaningful than to search for the ultimate meaning of life.

Dear friend,

Our mind doesn't have access to the ultimate meaning of life. Answers to questions about what the world is and how it was created can take us closer to the meaning. However, until we have a solid answer for the question of why the world was created, we will stay relatively ignorant.

Science has done a phenomenal job of answering the *what* and the *how*, but it hasn't moved an inch closer to answering the *why*. Knowledge that doesn't answer the *why* is limited. Awareness of the unimaginably large size of our universe (estimated at ninety-one billion light-years) creates a sense of awe—about the vastness of it all. Knowledge about the subatomic quantum world with awareness of the power of intentionality is truly fascinating. But the details of physics at both the cosmic and the quantum levels still leave the curious mind dissatisfied.

I believe the ultimate *why* (meaning) that will satisfy the human mind will be complete in itself, not depending on anything external to validate it. It will be resilient to the paradigm of life and death. I don't presently know how to reach that *why*.

I do, however, know how to align my limited mind with what I believe is my primary evolutionary responsibility—to help create a safer, happier, kinder world for our planet's children. Despite my good intentions, my personal ability to accomplish this goal is extraordinarily limited. I can influence only a minuscule part of the world in a very small way.

Minuscule, however, is better than nothing. If I procrastinate, waiting for the day when I have complete access to the global meaning or collect the resources to influence a large part of the world, I will reach nowhere.

I believe contextual, transient meanings all converge to a global meaning. If I can take hold of my own little meaning and pursue it to the deepest place it can take me, the reflection of the global meaning might reveal itself. That will be enough.

Questions of who created the sound and why aren't answerable. The immediate value comes in knowing how to turn the sound into music. Similarly, our minds in their current state of evolution cannot know who created the world or why. We can understand how to make the world a better place—one where we create more music than noise and also hear music behind the noise. And that is enough.

May you hear more music than noise; may you hear music behind the noise.

Take care.

Amit

* Suggested practice: Today, I will find the greatest meaning in helping the person in front of me.
(For additional practices, visit Stressfree.org/Immerse/)

Week 26

*D*uring this week you'll live your days fully listening to the voice of your conscience, and you'll be more accepting of yourself.

51. Conscience

Listen to the conscience, not just to the mind or the senses.

Dear friend,

Your entire repertoire of conscious experience comprises an integration of three inputs—sensory information from the world, sensory information from the body, and self-generated thoughts from the mind. At any instance, all of these inputs compete, and the information that is most salient (to survival value) becomes your present-moment experience. To simplify it further, in your entire life, your conscious present-moment experience will comprise either the input from the senses (external world or the body) or the thoughts generated by the mind.

Our five senses have no memory. They are passive conduits to the moment-by-moment flow of information. The mind uses the senses for safety, pleasure, and information.

The mind itself spontaneously churns countless thoughts and imaginations. These thoughts often project into a narrow time frame (usually yesterday, today, and tomorrow). The untrained mind mostly thinks thoughts related to self-worth, relationships, safety, and daily tasks.

If you live in a world where your physical safety is constantly threatened, external sensory input will likely dominate your conscious experience. This was the case for our ancestors, and it is true today in the war-torn or crime-prone areas. In the relatively safer parts of the world, where external dangers don't require diligence, your attention is free to roam in your mind, in the company of your thoughts and imaginations. Whether you know it or not, if you live in one of the safer neighborhoods, very likely, you spend the bulk of your day with your mind wandering. I believe this has created a unique opportunity for us.

When your attention is freed from the external threats and can focus inward, you have a choice—you can let your attention travel with spontaneous thoughts or direct it deeper, where conscience resides.

Conscience is the inner light that illumines the truth, telling me right from wrong. Conscience helps me do the right thing when no one is looking. My conscience isn't swayed by greed of pleasure or fear of pain. My conscience isn't selfish. It is objective, true, pure, and dependable. Conscience knows we all share the same sun and have the same *I*.

There is one problem though. Although conscience always has an opinion, it speaks in a humble, low volume, easily drowned by the vortices of the mind and the senses. When the majority of the world muffles the voice of conscience, we become unkind to each other.

I should dial up the volume of my conscience. I should use conscience as my guiding light. A mind anchored in conscience still experiences senses and thoughts. However, these thoughts and senses serve a self that includes many others. They help and heal, freeing the mind so it can fly into the vast vistas of the truth.

My mind is trainable. I should tether it to conscience so it can harness the senses, thoughts, words, and actions to comfort the other minds that are caught in the whirlpool of suffering. In that effort I will find peace and freedom.

May your conscience speak louder than your senses and thoughts; may your ears listen to your conscience more than they listen to your desires.

Take care.

Amit

* Suggested practice: Today, I will remind myself several times that I am a good human being and that any unethical thought, word, or action is unbecoming of me.
(For additional practices, visit Stressfree.org/Immerse/)

52. Love Yourself

❧

Can you look at yourself differently?

Dear friend,

You are the only *you* there ever was or will be. Even identical twins have different fingerprints and subtle differences in their genetic makeup due to acquired changes (caused by epigenetic modifications and mutations). The probability that any two individuals will have identical genetic makeup is so low (less than one in several hundred trillion or less) as to be practically impossible.

Despite the differences, our similarities are overwhelming. Our physical bodies all have the same basic design, both external and internal. We share all the essential organs—brain, heart, liver, kidneys, and more—and also the not-so-essential (called vestigial) organs—appendix, tail bone, wisdom teeth, muscles that move the ears, and others. Your heart and kidney cells will look similar to mine under the microscope. Nevertheless, we are designed to notice our differences more than our similarities.

We notice our slanting teeth, unique noses, splintered nails, moles, and wrinkles. We give our peculiarities judgmental adjectives—the crooked teeth, the bulbous nose, the cracking nails, the hideous mole, the unsightly wrinkle. On days we find enough of these, we would rather duck under the covers than face the world.

Similarly, when we think about our past, we don't dwell on the fifty thousand meals we ate or the 146,000 hours we slept (for an average fifty-year-old). Instead, we think about our unique experiences—the people we dated, the love we shared, the love we missed or withheld, the places we visited, the pranks we regret (doing or not doing!).

Why do we focus so much on differences? The answer is simple— what unites us we perceive as old news—boring and unworthy of attention. What makes us unique is interesting and draws our senses. Given our negativity bias, unique traits, although interesting, are vulnerable to negative judgment. That's where you can make a change. Your choice of how you look at your uniqueness can have a profound impact on your self-worth and vitality.

You have three choices in how you look at your uniqueness—passively, with self-loathing, or with self-love. If you leave it to default the former two will prevail. With passivity or self-loathing, you won't know how to collect the warmth the world sends your way. You won't return that warmth either. Life will desiccate that way.

The alternative is self-love. Self-love doesn't mean being haughty or arrogant or living in blissful indifference. Self-love is self-kindness. When you love yourself, you give the spark of life traveling within you a more memorable experience. You don't abandon it to dwell on doubts, hurts, hates, envies, or sorrows. You focus it on gratitude, compassion, admiration, and hope. You don't look at your countenance or complexion and call it ugly. You accept and embrace yourself as you are.

If you aren't afraid to show your love to a six-month-old who smiles at you with her big, blue eyes from her stroller in the grocery check-out line, don't be afraid of loving yourself. You were the same adorable six-month-old a few years ago. You then trusted the love that came your way and smiled back. By loving her, you don't spoil her; you show you care. You let her know that she is worthy of your attention. She reminds you of all that is good about life, that there is hope.

When you connect with her and exchange smiles, you experience the joy of being unconditionally accepted.

I'm sure you like to be in a party where you are being accepted, appreciated, and admired, and not rejected or hated. The same is true for the spark of life within you. When it finds a party within you, it will join in the fun and stay until very late. Otherwise, it might call it quits, and who knows where it will go seeking self-love. Don't let that happen.

May you never forget loving yourself; may you help others remember loving themselves.

Take care.

Amit

* Suggested practice: Today, I will pay greater attention to the most attractive aspects of my physical appearance.
(For additional practices, visit Stressfree.org/Immerse/)

Week 27

*D*uring this week you'll seek what is right in the other person, and you'll find greater novelty in people and experiences that might otherwise have felt familiar and ordinary.

53. Blame Game

Validate before blaming.

Dear friend,

Research shows we don't see what our eyes see; we see what our brain thinks we are seeing. Our brain tells our eyes what it wants to see, and when the eyes obey, the brain believes what they show. From among many possibilities, we thus see, hear, and believe the details that confirm our preset beliefs.

Our beliefs guide our preferences. Our preferences direct our words and actions, which eventually shape our life. How and what we see thus are very important to our lives and those of others who depend on us.

Interestingly, most of us aren't aware that we are so biased. We are oblivious to our blind spots; we believe we are rational. Not realizing that our truth is just one aspect of the complete truth, we become anchored in our version. Our truth becomes an integral part of our being. Defending it becomes our mission, even at the risk of creating conflicts with the world.

Conflicts happen when both sides perceive being wronged and intend to right that wrong. In conflicts, the two parties protect different versions of the truth. In this state, each is blind and deaf to why the other person sees and hears what he or she sees and hears.

We can avoid conflicts once we realize that our individual truth is just one version of reality, not necessarily the right or complete version. When I stand rigid on my post, most others look unreasonable. Realizing this, I should change my default assumption from "you are wrong and I am right" (or "you are right and I am wrong," as can happen to people with low self-esteem) to "we both could be right."

I believe I have the ability to make this change. I have the ability to change my anxiety-provoking negative bias to goodness-seeking positive bias. Research shows that once we bias ourselves to "seek" the positive, we start "finding" more positive. As a result, we develop more positive emotions, better social connections, and greater prosocial behavior.

I should recognize my negativity bias. With that recognition, I should strive to overcome this bias by seeking what is right in others.

With that disposition I will default to peace. And when we all look at each other and seek what is right in the other person, the world will default to peace.

May the world notice the good within you; may you notice the good in the world.

Take care.

Amit

*   Suggested practice: Today, I will honor others' constraints before I judge them.
(For additional practices, visit Stressfree.org/Immerse/)

54. Pancakes

Each moment is fresh and novel.

Dear friend,

Weekday breakfasts are perhaps the most neglected meal of the day. We often skip breakfast or swallow the bagels like alligators—eating without tasting. Breakfast, when it happens, is often a speedy intake of calories, caffeine, and information. We seldom savor, think, or connect during this time. Our job profiles that entail less manual and more cognitive labor require us to be focused and awake, rather than dulled by cereal deluge. This habit of hurrying, which is understandably the norm on the weekdays, often carries into the weekend.

"Can I have one more pancake, please?" I heard myself say at the breakfast table on one of the weekends. "I am still hungry. The first pancake I sort of ate in a hurry and didn't enjoy as much."

I resolved to savor the second one a bit more. Lucky for me, there was still some mix left in the bowl.

I thought about my life. I may have experienced its earlier moments in a hurry—I was pressed for time, struggling, wishing to succeed. The world was unkind, and I didn't know better. Fortunately for me, there is still opportunity.

I need to realize that someday the mix will be gone. I want to get up satisfied from the table (a life lived with deeper meaning). I also have finite days when I will get to eat.

I need to remember that what I consider the second helping is actually the first. No two pancakes are exactly alike. I should eat each of them with equal novelty, just as the tenth patient in a row I see as a doctor with a sore throat is still novel, if not for me, certainly for him or her.

I should also eat the first pancake as if it is my second and the final one for the day.

May you remember to savor your moments; may you have plentiful moments to savor.

Take care.

Amit

* Suggested practice: Today, I will meet at least one colleague or neighbor as a long-lost friend.

(For additional practices, visit Stressfree.org/Immerse/)

Week 28

uring this week you'll recognize and honor the sacred within each be-ing, and you'll seek the good, not necessarily the pleasant.

55. Precious and Meaningful

Every stranger could have been your friend or loved one.

Dear friend,

SNR 172. I don't know if this means anything to you—perhaps a user ID, a password, a bank locker number, or even an acronym. It meant nothing to me either until it was assigned as the license-plate number for our car in 2010. Now I see it almost every day. It is mine in some ways, with my safety linked to the safety of the vehicle that carries this plate.

How many things or people are potentially linked to me that I presently don't know? Their meaning will manifest at some future point. As I pick my four-year-old up from day care, how can I not help but be thankful to the family of her lovely teacher, who gives her so much love, care, and patience, despite her personal medical challenges. I feel deeply connected to my daughter's teacher's parents, even though I haven't ever met them. Perhaps a doctor who might save my life in the future was just born today. Presently I don't know that child, that child's parents, someone who might inspire him or her to study hard, or any of his or her teachers.

If I extend this imagination, everybody and everything become relevant and meaningful to me. Nothing is an exception. Every stranger could be my friend, colleague, or loved one. Everybody is special, worthy of my attention and kindness.

I have no doubt that one or many of you, through some benign act, has profoundly helped me, perhaps even saved my life or those of my loved ones. When I live my day today thinking such, I feel more grateful and connected to you. Every day that I am alive and can take a deep breath, I should carry this belief. This awareness will give me greater peace, joy, and vitality.

Live your day today keeping the conviction that everyone and everything around you are precious and meaningful, and they are helping you more than you can imagine.

May you find a deeper connection with others, remembering that each person is connected with your life in ways you don't even know.

Take care.

Amit

* Suggested practice: Today, I will consider each person as part of my ancestry tree.
  (For additional practices, visit Stressfree.org/Immerse/)

56. Pleasant and Good

Good isn't always pleasant.

Dear friend,

Our minds love to marinate in the pleasant, addicted as they are to short-term gratifications. If that were not the case, we wouldn't find calorie-dense food irresistible, a proportion of us wouldn't cheat in marriage, and a search for tax evasion or corporate fraud on the Internet would produce zero links. The pleasant served by sensory experiences alone, however, is hollow. Pleasantness bereft of goodness is as nourishing as a bowl of sugar. It can't provide lasting fulfillment. The pleasant provides lasting pleasure only when flavored with the good.

Based on whether they are pleasant and/or good, life's experiences can be divided into four categories:

* Good and pleasant;
* Good and unpleasant;
* Not-good and pleasant;
* Not-good and unpleasant.

Most of us easily avoid the not-good that is unpleasant (e.g., mosquito bites) and seek the good that is pleasant (e.g., quality time with loved ones).

The real struggle is embracing the good that can be unpleasant (e.g., exercise, paying taxes) while avoiding the pleasant that is not so good (e.g., calorie-dense food). This is a tall order for the mind that struggles with distracted attention, willpower depletion, and the allure of supernormal, irresistible sensory stimuli in the present world that would have totally floored the kings of the yesteryears.

Before asking ourselves to pursue the good, we should first define what we mean by *good*. There isn't a single definition. Good is what we pursue to realize our highest potential. Good helps us create a world where our children can thrive. Good is collective and prosocial. Good is patient. Good gives out compassion. Good is powered by gratitude. Good serves a meaning higher than itself.

I need freedom from my mind's predispositions—its fears, selfishness, and sensory cravings—so I can sample the good. I need freedom so my mind can dig deeper and hear the voice of the conscience. I surrender to the reality—that my mind is ignorant. In that surrender I find hope. I see the light coming from the invisible past. I see philosophers, scientists, poets, seekers, and patriotic citizens who threaded the path of the good, happily sacrificing the pleasant. Here is what I hear them say:

If you want to pursue the good—

* Do what is right for the planet's children.
* Live a value- and meaning-driven life.

* Think of others as you think about yourself.
* Do what is right for the country.
* Be kind.
* Forgive.
* Be humble and gentle.
* Praise.
* Listen.

I must tether my mind to one of these ideas if I hope to resist my mind's temptations. The one I like the most today is, "Do what is right for the planet's children." I have found most of my conflicts melt away when I subject my cravings or indecisions to this question.

I should intentionally seek the good until it becomes innate to me. And if I do that with all my sincerity, I might leave a trail for the unborn, who will wake up one day determined to barter the pleasant for the good.

May you find the pleasant in the good; may you find the good in the prosocial.

Take care.

Amit

* Suggested practice: Today, I will do the right thing, whether or not it is pleasant.
(For additional practices, visit Stressfree.org/Immerse/)

Week 29

*D*uring this week you'll be grateful for the simple and the mundane, and you'll serve the world in a selfless way.

57. Gratitude Threshold

Can I lower my gratitude threshold?

Dear friend,

This year I have gone through three pairs of shoes already. The first one fit perfectly well when I bought it, but starting the very next day, it made my right little toe sore. The second one also fit perfectly but created an embarrassing noise (like Velcro rubbing) when I walked on the hard-wood or tiled floor. (I often found people pulling their eyes off their smartphones when I walked past them.) The third pair seems like a perfect match—it causes no pain and no noise, and it feels feather-weight. The third pair is also the one I have noticed the least. When my shoes bothered me, I noticed them a lot. Now that they sit comfortably on my feet, I have forgotten all about them.

I realize that, like most of us, I don't recognize my comforts. My best gloves are the ones I don't feel once I wear them. Expanding on this thought, I have seldom if ever thought about the trillions of cells that collaborate and connect to create my kidneys, liver, gallbladder, heart, and many other organs, which are quietly doing their job, keeping me alive and well, and gifting me with conscious experience.

As a result, not only do I not feel things and body parts that are working well and not hurting, but I also do not fully appreciate the infinite value of friends, loved ones, and colleagues who support me. I believe that's a big loss.

I can only truly know how much I want or need someone or something that I already have in my life by losing it. I don't wish to wait for that day. I have the power to imagine the loss, and powered with that insight, I can choose to perceive the simple as simply special. If I don't, life will pass me by as I snooze in ignorant stupor, waking up only when stranded in pain.

While I can't live my entire day just thanking the stars, I can stop every once in a while and be grateful for a deep breath, the taste of pure water, the smell of fresh grass, the slurp of noodles, and the smile of a loved one. I should also be grateful that I have the ability to be grateful. Not doing so means missing out on life.

May gratitude always keep you company, amid comfort and success as well as pain and failure.

Take care.

Amit

* Suggested practice: Today, I will be grateful for all aspects of nature that surround me—green grass, trees, blue sky, dirt.
(For additional practices, visit Stressfree.org/Immerse/)

58. The Tree Teacher

Assume the consciousness of a tree to attain the ultimate wisdom.

Dear friend,

I want to be like a tree. I want to grow toward the light and give shelter to the birds, shade to the tired, medicine to the sick, fuel to the needy, air to the living, and fruit to the hungry.

I want to produce flowers that spread fragrance farther from my physical form. I want to bend with humility when I am lush with fruits. When someone throws a rock at me, I want to have the poise and grace to send back a fruit in return. I want to anchor the soil and work with my fellow trees to pacify the storms so they unleash less anger. I want to control the noise and improve a neighborhood's beauty.

Having lived a full life, when I pass away, I wish my physical body to still serve others. I wish to continue to hear until eternity babies being born, children laughing and running, and men and women talking words of wisdom and kindness.

I want every part of me to be useful. If I could be like a tree even for a single day, I would consider myself blessed.

May you be surrounded by trees; may the trees around you inspire you.

Take care.

Amit

* Suggested practice: Today, I will accept life's winter as time to shed leaves and exercise patience so I can bloom again in life's spring. (For additional practices, visit Stressfree.org/Immerse/)

Week 30

During this week you'll appreciate your connectedness with others and commit to remaining hopeful despite getting stuck in difficult circumstances.

59. Vending Machine

The world isn't a vending machine; it is our cosmic mother.

Dear friend,

Evolutionary biologists teach us that we are inclined to behave most selflessly toward those who are genetically closest to us. In the din of a penguin colony, a mama penguin can recognize her baby's call from among thousands of penguins. Every tracker knows to never come between a female bear and her cubs.

At a recent wedding festivity overseas, it was painful to watch hungry street kids being shunned while the hosts eagerly overfed the invited guests. We often lavishly spend for our kids' activities but hesitate to help an equally worthy child with a different last name. I share the same predisposition.

I have a very narrow definition of me and mine. Everyone else belongs to a less important category—"the others." I don't like anyone hurt, but my compassion toward the unfamiliar "others" is embarrassingly low. I forget that the "others" are me and mine with a different face and different locus. They aren't cows to be milked. They are sentient and precious.

I should try to transcend my biological predisposition to be compassionate toward only a few. Expanding my zone of compassion doesn't mean I will give everything away. World hunger is too deep for my tiny hands to make any dent. Expanding my zone means I will be considerate of others. I will carry an intention to help at least one person in need. If all of us take care of just one more person, our world will bypass most of its suffering.

The world we live in isn't a vending machine where I can collect goodies by pressing buttons. The world is my ultimate provider. The world isn't because of me; I am because the world is. We are in it together. And if I wish to thrive, I need to feed the world and honor others as much as I wish to be fed and honored.

May you live in a world filled with love; may the love in your world be defined by compassion.

Take care.

Amit

* Suggested practice: Today, I will appreciate and honor each person helping me, directly or indirectly.
(For additional practices, visit Stressfree.org/Immerse/)

60. Hope

The sun will always rise, no matter what.

Dear friend,

Astronomers estimate that each day approximately 275 million stars are born. Our galaxy alone has 200 to 400 billion stars. With over 100 billion galaxies in the universe, many believe the universe has more stars than the number of sand particles on all the earth's beaches combined. We, of course, have to be content with owning just one star—our sun.

Our sun sits at the perfect distance from the earth (about ninety-three million miles) to give us a toasty existence without frying us with its six-thousand-kelvin surface temperature. Depending on where you live and the month of the year, the sun lights up the sky for a part of the day. When the sun turns its back at night, countless candles, lights, and lamps illumine our homes, using the energy we absorbed from the sun.

The sun and the lamps fulfill each other's purpose. The sun is the source; the lamps continue to distribute its light when the sun is busy elsewhere.

None of us is the sun. But we all can be lamps. I believe that's what the world needs—countless lamps, so the night will never be dark.

My life, driven by this purpose, will help me come out of my darkness.

My humble light, weak as it is, can still inspire hope so others can make it through the dark, keeping their eyes open, as I do, waiting for the sunrise, which always happens no matter how dark the night may have been.

May the sun rise for you each morning; may your eyes be open to see the rising sun each morning.

Take care.

Amit

*   Suggested practice: Today, I will assume my adversities have a meaning, even if I can't see it.
(For additional practices, visit Stressfree.org/Immerse/)

Week 31

During this week you'll reframe previous suffering and recognize that even those who seem unkind may have helped you and may have something to teach you.

61. Compassion and Suffering

Let suffering, personal or witnessed, evoke compassion, until you reach a point where your compassion is spontaneous without the need for suffering.

Dear friend,

Suffering, personal or witnessed, often leaves a residue. That residue could be a painful scar that invades many future conscious moments. This scar takes away hope, crushes trust, and makes you fearful and paranoid. An event of suffering thus can seed a lifetime of unhappiness. Different names capture this ongoing suffering—post-traumatic stress disorder, chronic stress, battle fatigue, burnout, and more.

The residue could also lead to a changed worldview. One engages with life in all its richness and becomes gentler and more patient. Relationships improve, priorities change, and newer possibilities emerge. This new perspective recognizes each moment without suffering as precious and transient. One becomes stronger and more resilient to future suffering. Such resilience doesn't lead one back to just the baseline; it raises the baseline—one grows as a result of the tumble. No wonder some experts call this phenomenon post-traumatic growth.

It is important to recognize that trauma itself doesn't lead to growth. Trauma wakes up the individual to recruit greater inner resources and develop a more mature viewpoint to start on the growth trajectory. Further, growth itself doesn't guarantee an end to pain; growth and pain often coexist, although the pain amid growth feels more tolerable.

How can you "choose" the growth trajectory? The more intentional you are about how you look at your adversity, particularly in its early, delicate phase, the greater the likelihood of growth. Learning to find the right within the wrong, accepting that some adversities are part of life, and trying to find meaning in adversity are useful first steps. Having caring people around you who are willing to listen and provide a wise counsel greatly helps.

Adversity-stimulated growth preserves hope. Such growth doesn't let adversity diminish the light of compassion within you. Adversity kindles stronger compassion.

Initially, such compassion extends only to those one knows are suffering. Gradually one breaks this barrier and recognizes that the list of suffering people includes everyone, even those who may have knowingly or unknowingly caused suffering.

That land is blessed where compassion thrives without the personal experience of suffering. Most places on earth, however, need suffering to evoke compassion.

Suffering that doesn't evoke compassion may not fulfill its potential purpose. We should create a world where compassion sprouts without the need for suffering. Until we reach there, let suffering create, not a scar, but a mind that is willing to give and receive kindness.

May you suffer less; may your suffering make you stronger and kinder.

Take care.

Amit

*   Suggested practice: Today, I will recognize that an expression other than love often is a call for help.
(For additional practices, visit Stressfree.org/Immerse/)

62. Bad and Good

Good and bad depend on context.

Dear friend,

Despite my unflinching commitment to honor life, as a physician, I have witnessed untold agony where death seemed the preferred alternative. Severe pain or unremitting nausea unresponsive to the strongest medications in a patient with terminal cancer is difficult to watch. I and the patient's loved ones have sometimes been relieved with the liberation. What most would consider an undesirable option (death) can occasion relief, depending on what preceded it. Good and bad aren't absolute; they are relative to the unique context.

What I seek this moment depends on the context. I seek cool shade in summers and hot chocolate in winters. Depending on the rest of my cards, the jack of spades may be worth nothing or may win me the hand.

Further, with the infinite possibilities that each moment hides, good and bad coexist—in each experience. What seems good in the near term may become hurtful with the passage of time. The human mind can't discern the eventual impact of any event—the known and the unknown are too many, and how they will eventually interact is beyond anyone's comprehension.

Despite knowing all of this at an intellectual level, I can't shed my tendency to categorize events as either good or bad. I am forever seeking the pleasant (which my mind assumes is good) and evading the unpleasant (which my mind assumes is bad).

I accept defeat, for my mind can't escape the duality of good and bad. Instead, while I continue to seek the good and the pleasant, I accept that my inbox will always have some unpleasant that is bad. Over time, I might be able to sift them. I might be able to send the unpleasant that is bad into the recycle bin. That time, however, hasn't arrived yet.

I don't crave the bad, but I can choose to be grateful that my bad isn't as bad as it could have been. Also I can keep the hope that the bad might turn into good in the blink of an eye. Gratitude and hope help me accept the bad. The bad that is shamed and fought can become toxic. My humble hope is that the bad that is accepted, and reminded of its potential for good, will turn into good.

May your hope for a better future and gratitude for the good within the bad help you accept and transform the bad.

Take care.

Amit

*   Suggested practice: Today, I will be grateful that my bad perhaps isn't as bad as it could have been.
(For additional practices, visit Stressfree.org/Immerse/)

Week 32

*D*uring this week you'll actively avoid hatred, envy, revenge, and anger (HERA), and you'll find a better way to eat sour mangoes.

63. Do Not Hurt Yourself

Do not let hatred, envy, revenge, or anger (HERA) stay in any corner of your being.

Dear friend,

Hera was the wife and sister of Zeus, the sky and thunder god in ancient Greek religion. Hera was known for her jealousy and vengeance, which came partly as a reaction to Zeus's infidelity. The difficulties Hera faced weren't unique to her life or her times. Many of us face difficult interpersonal situations that awaken a different Hera within us—the Hera of **Hatred**, **Envy**, **Revenge**, and **Anger** (the anger that produces violent rage). Research shows this HERA predisposes us to a multitude of medical conditions.

Just as a physical body fighting an external infectious agent becomes inflamed and injured, and a country at war finds it difficult to keep its citizens peaceful, when we intend to hurt others—either because they hurt us or because we feel hatred or envy—we hurt ourselves. Research shows a mind fighting itself or others predisposes the physical body to cardiovascular disease, cancer, infections, inflammation, dementia, and even premature death. In one of my workshops on forgiveness, a participant got up in the middle and said, "I can't give my ex the power to increase my risk of dementia. That's a good enough reason to forgive him, as much as I hate to do that."

The other reason HERA damages our system is that once we are mired in the habit of getting angry, feeling hatred, harboring envy, or seeking revenge with one person, we deploy these missiles to the rest of the world. We paint the world with our negativity and seek out reasons to validate our inner negative feelings. These feelings start defining our life's course. Locked in the HERA prison, we start despising the world, jeopardizing our peace and even our very existence.

HERA often sneaks in from an unguarded corner of the mind, when you aren't watching. It then multiplies, like a newly hatched virus against which you have no immunity. Carefully guard your mind—not just its living room, but also its attic, basement, and backyard—from any elements of HERA and sweep it clean when you find these hatching. Crowd your space with the antidotes—gratitude, compassion, and forgiveness. Transform your negative thoughts so they surrender to these higher values.

When you convert your hatred into compassion, envy into inspiration, revenge into forgiveness, and anger into acceptance, you'll save yourself and the people you love from much suffering.

May you create a beautiful day by sweeping your mind clean of any hatred, envy, revenge, and anger.

Take care.

Amit

* Suggested practice: Today, I will be compassionate toward myself if I am not able to fully shed hatred, envy, revenge, and anger. (For additional practices, visit Stressfree.org/Immerse/)

64. Sweet Mangoes

How to deal with difficult people

Dear friend,

I have had a very long love affair with mangoes. Yet I can't always tell the sweet ones from the sour. Color isn't always a good guide. Some mangoes are perfectly ripe when green; others turn yellow, orange, or red by the time their mealy starches turn into simple sugars. Fragrance and consistency are a bit more reliable. A perfectly ripe one often has an appetizing, sweet fragrance, particularly near the stem end. A mango turning from firm to soft also provides a helpful hint.

Of all the tests, however, the most definitive is the obvious one—eat a slice. I either taste heaven or regret the loss of a dollar.

My most common response to a sour mango is to escort it to the garbage can, wash my mouth, and try the next one, hoping it will be lush with fructose. I keep trying until I find one that is willing to pamper my palate.

I wonder if our relationships are also like that. Many of your colleagues, friends, and loved ones are sweet, but some are definitely sour. You can't spot the sour ones ahead of time. When you face such people, you minimize the time you spend with them, try your best so they don't linger in your mind, and as soon as the opportunity presents itself, move on to someone sweeter.

But what to do with those sour ones you cannot avoid? They may be close family members or neighbors. If you are hungry and have nothing but sour mangoes to eat, what are you going to do? Here is what I do.

I sprinkle the slices with sugar or honey. I know the sour taste won't go away, but I'll feel less of it. The slices become more palatable. Most manufacturers of syrupy preparations for children know this trick very well.

On sour people you sprinkle the honey of gratitude, compassion, acceptance, and forgiveness, recognizing and knowing fully well that their inherent nature is unlikely to change.

I wish the world was perfect and every mango was fully ripe. But the world isn't perfect, and none of us will escape facing sour specimens. With over four hundred varieties of mangoes on the market, I will run into the unpleasant ones once in a while. My only option is to avoid the sour mangoes best I can, savor the sweet, ripe ones, and if I'm faced with a sour one that I can't avoid, sprinkle some sugar or honey on it.

May you have few or no difficult people in your life; may the difficult people not usurp your hope or lower your values.

Take care.

Amit

*   Suggested practice: Today, I will keep my focus on my higher meaning as I deal with difficult people.
(For additional practices, visit Stressfree.org/Immerse/)

Week 33

During this week you'll seek to transform your vulnerabilities so they serve a higher meaning, and you'll turn your envy into inspiration.

65. Balance

Harness your fear, greed, and selfishness to serve the world.

Dear friend,

As much as I would like to live an ethical, moral life, I struggle with three of my mind's predispositions—fear, greed, and selfishness.

I have heard of ideal love that knows no fear—I am not there yet. I have heard of ideal want that seeks only the pious and the just—I am not that altruistic. I have heard of total selflessness—I don't think

I will reach that ideal in this lifetime. I must face the truth. I must accept that I will have fear, greed, and selfishness until the last breath.

This acceptance relieves me. It provides me the perspective to help me redirect my predispositions. "Why shouldn't I harness my vulnerabilities to enrich my life?" I ask myself.

Why can't I feel greedy about helping many, fear that I might close my life without meaningfully serving a small corner of the world, and be selfish about growing emotionally and spiritually through becoming a kinder human being?

I believe when my fear, greed, and selfishness surrender to serve of a higher purpose, they will lose their sting. They will then thrive in a state of balance.

That balance for fear means being appropriately cautious—neither frozen in panic nor negligent. For greed it means being fittingly passionate—neither marinated in wants nor apathetic. With selfishness, balance means being pragmatically altruistic—neither egoistic and self-centered nor impractically selfless.

The outcome is that you become fear-less, desire-less, and self-less (not zero fear, desire, or selfishness, but less of it) and thus save tremendous energy to become an agent of service and love.

May you become fear-less, desire-less, and self-less; may you harness your fear, desire, and selfishness to serve a higher purpose.

Take care.

Amit

* Suggested practice: Today, I will let go of one irrational fear. (For additional practices, visit Stressfree.org/Immerse/)

66. Put Envy to Work

Envy can inspire you into excellence.

Dear friend,

I have turned red with embarrassment, blue with melancholy, yellow with cowardice, gray with boredom, pink with happiness, purple with relaxation, and white with fear. Of all the colors, the one I am least proud of is turning green with envy.

Envy is the pain I get from seeing others' joy. Envy means wanting what the other person has, wishing he or she didn't have it, and willing or inflicting harm to him or her. In envy, I have experienced the first two, and I hope I never experience the third one.

Envy originates in our mind's nature to compare. The magic mirror on the wall won't forever call you the fairest in every aspect of life. Further, when you look around and see the disproportionate distribution of material goods, success, and other worldly things, you will conclude that the world isn't fair. Effort isn't always rewarded, and laziness or bad intentions aren't always punished. Bad things happen to good people, and good things happen to bad people. Envy is thus natural.

My envy is my prison. Envy makes me empty and blind—depleted of positive emotions and blinded to my own blessings. Envy demoralizes me. I quit my efforts, feel like a victim, become resentful, and sink into apathy. The green of envy also can easily turn into more sinister colors, making me aggressive and insensitive and depersonalizing the other person in my mind. Many wrongful, unthinkable acts have happened in this state.

A parallel sentiment to feeling pain in others' joy is feeling joy in others' pain. When you are attracted to the news showing the fall from grace of someone rich and famous, you experience "suffer entertainment," also called schadenfreude. When we read negative press about someone we envy, we activate our brain's pleasure center. While we may quickly recover our righteousness, I have no doubt the pleasure centers in your brain and mine regularly participate in suffer entertainment.

It doesn't have to be this way. If I choose, seeing suffering can evoke compassion in me, and feeling envious can inspire me. Here are seven ideas to help envy inspire you:

* Validate others' hard work—Look deeper and search for reasons why someone else received more than you did. Often, you'll discover tremendous hard work (with, of course, a side helping of luck).
* Remember and be grateful for your blessings—Before you get envious, be grateful that without knowing or trying, you may have received countless gifts from the world. We don't know why one child is orphaned from birth while another gets pampered by hundreds. We can only be grateful for the love and nurturing we have received.
* Recognize others' suffering—Most people are good at hiding their pain. While you see material success, you seldom can see the daily emotional struggles. Assume that most people

are struggling—even the ones who look perfectly balanced and cheerful, who seem to have it all.

* Minimize comparisons—Every person has his or her strong domain. Honor individual strengths and be kind to individual weaknesses.

* Focus on self-improvement—When you see others doing well, instead of labeling it unjust or getting into the victim mode, use that as an inspiration to improve yourself. Wish for yourself without unwishing for others.

* Change your seeking—Instead of seeking just material success or fame, seek the virtues you gain from good deeds and altruistic intentions. Be envious that the other person is helping so many, and get inspired to rise to that level or higher.

Ignoring envy won't help. Envy is instinctive, and it's often the first response to seeing someone's success. Recognize its nature and learn how the glitter of the world attracts the mind. Harness envy to inspire you toward a more meaning-filled life. Never let envy translate into inflicting harm on others or feeling joy in others' pain. Finally, remain humble and kind so your success doesn't create envy in others, recognizing that your humility and kindness may still not protect you, as perhaps Snow White could tell you.

With deeper insights when you truly shed your envy, you'll find the space filled with love, to which the space truly belongs.

May you be inspired into doing good by others' success and into humility by your own success.

Take care.

Amit

*   Suggested practice: Today, I will focus more on others' hard work than their success.

(For additional practices, visit Stressfree.org/Immerse/)

Week 34

During this week you'll prioritize compassion over fear or unhealthy desire, and you'll treat every person and every object with greater respect.

67. The Enemy of Compassion Is...

Let go of fear, if you wish to be compassionate.

Dear friend,

We were visiting Orlando, Florida. A bus pulled up to drop off a few passengers. A girl, about eight years old, didn't seem too well. As she was coming out, right before exiting, she threw up. The floor was littered with food. Everyone took four steps back. Suddenly she had become untouchable. I could see fear in people's eyes. "Is she infectious...What if she has E. coli...I hope I don't get that bug...I need to watch my kids." Amid perception of personal threat, we all closed in.

Meanwhile, the girl's elderly grandmother, with much effort, picked her up and took her out of the bus. People covered their noses, repulsed by the secretions.

Do you know what was missing? Compassion.

Fear and disgust dominated our minds, not compassion for the little girl—we were too fearful to be compassionate. Fearful of what? The child had just mild food poisoning. She would be fine in a day or two. She wasn't even infectious. The experience taught me a lesson.

The first barrier to compassion is fear. I fear that I might get hurt. I fear that my compassion will be misjudged. I fear that my compassion might not help. I fear I will be too stretched. When I am lost in personal "what ifs," I am unavailable for compassion.

Two types of fear hurt compassion. First is the fear of the person. This fear may occur because of potential harm from the person—intentional or unintentional. Fear provokes self-protective thoughts and actions that totally crowd one's mind and leave no bandwidth for any other thought. The second type is fear of compassion itself. Why should that be?

People fear compassion for many reasons. Some get distressed at seeing others' suffering and thus avoid it. Some feel compelled to follow the group norm and try to fit in if it doesn't support compassion. Others may think compassion enables bad behavior. A few have been hurt by prior acts of compassion. Those involved in caring professions or who have seen a lot of suffering may develop compassion fatigue. Finally are those who feel their compassion will deplete their resources; finite as their energy is, they wish to use it only for the people closest to them (those who can reciprocate their compassion).

When we fear giving out compassion to others, we struggle with receiving it from them. We also are unable to be compassionate toward the self. We feel less worthy and call out compassion as weakness. We also fear that if we are kind and nonjudgmental to the self, then something bad will happen.

I need to overcome these barriers. I wish to be compassionate toward myself, to trust the compassion the world sends me, and to send compassion back to the world in return. The first step is to be compassionate toward myself, by believing that I deserve compassion.

I need to believe that I am fulfilling an important meaning that the world cares about. I need to believe that I am a kind human being. I need to pick a small part of the world and invest my time and resources to make it a little happier and more hopeful than I found it. If I am able to do that, I will not feel like an imposter in my world. Once I am self-compassionate, I will be a better receiver of the compassion sent to me, and thus I will have extra energy. That will allow me not to see compassion as depleting and be fearful of it, but to wake up each day and generously give out my compassion.

Cultivate compassion by relinquishing fear. It will give you more joy than you can ever imagine.

May you not fear compassion; may compassion remove your fears.

Take care.

Amit

* Suggested practice: Today, I will assume that the person who annoys me has struggles similar to my own.
(For additional practices, visit Stressfree.org/Immerse/)

68. Selfie with a Tulip

Try to find the extraordinary within the ordinary, if you wish to change the world around you.

Dear friend,

I was wondering one day—what if the moon rose once every hundred years; wouldn't I be awake all night looking at it? What if the flowers bloomed once in my lifetime; wouldn't I be taking selfies with the tulips? I don't, because my mind perceives each of these spectacles as ordinary.

The ordinary is perceived as ordinary because my senses and mind have become used to it. I define extraordinary if it defies the natural law or is rare. Who has the authority to define the natural law? To a Neanderthal, the space shuttle would be a miracle, as would open-heart surgery. Our four-year-old routinely flatters me with, "Dad, how did you do that?" when I lift twenty pounds or scale four feet in one jump. To her, these feats are miraculous. Isn't everything then extraordinary, at least from someone's perspective?

A normal EKG may be a boring sight to an experienced cardiologist, but for a fifty-year-old man with chest pain, that normal EKG is extraordinarily comforting. An empty, dirty bowl in the sink isn't particularly attractive, but if it shows that your child who is recovering from a severe illness has had her first full meal, the empty bowl is a divine sight.

This drop of water may have quenched a thirsty baby, nourished a hungry plant, or saved a dried-out cactus. Its next stop may power a great thought that could save the world. I should revere this drop as it touches my skin, lips, or hair. Each drop is precious. So is each pound of dirt, every rock, every cloud, each seed.

Looking at the inanimate as precious helps you treat everything around you with greater respect. Further, once you train yourself to find the inanimate precious, you become attuned to finding the animate precious. The man in front of you isn't a means to an end. He is a dad, hubby, son, brother, friend, cousin, grandkid, neighbor, and colleague. He has helped many and has struggled with self-esteem and worries.

Expanding your imagination, you can think about how far he has traveled to be with you and where he will go after he drives on. This moment with him is precious, worthy of your full attention. When you stitch several of these moments together, you create your day. When you find meaning in what is in front of you, your days join together to gift you a life full of meaning.

You realize that every person is a product of a series of miracles— conception, the joining of two cells; rapid multiplication to create an embryo and then a fetus; growth of a heart, brain, and all the rest using a genetic blueprint; and then the miracle of childbirth, which changes lungs from solid to hollow structures and moves the fetus from the confines of the womb and dependence on the placenta to an independent existence. The infinite series of events that precede a child's birth is a true miracle.

Let the noise inside your head, that of a busy life, not blur your eyes to everyday miracles or drown the quiet of your heart. Let technology, instead of becoming the primary distraction, free up your attention for deeper experience of the world and inspire kinder, more prosocial thoughts and nobler pursuits. Find the ordinary as precious, even miraculous.

Look at the moon today as if it were the first time you were seeing it. And there is nothing wrong in taking a selfie with the tulips.

Find the extraordinary within the ordinary.

Take care.

Amit

*   Suggested practice: Today, I will be gentle with all objects around me. (For additional practices, visit Stressfree.org/Immerse/)

Week 35

*D*uring this week you'll lower your threshold for happiness and learn to focus your energy on your effort without getting anxious about the outcome.

69. Our First Flight

The lower your threshold to be content, the greater meaning you will fulfill.

Dear friend,

My first flying experience was a one-hour flight as a newly married twenty-six-year-old. We got clumsy with the seat belt, didn't know how to open the overhead bin, and annoyed the elderly gentleman sitting next to us with our ignorant giggles, as we discovered a new world at thirty-six thousand feet. Like three-year-olds, we were seeking fun rather than looking for imperfections.

The novelty has worn off now, for us as well as others. As a result, we have started looking for imperfections.

A few months ago, during a two-hour flight, I was sitting alongside a busy-looking gentleman. He seemed visibly upset. I didn't hear any curse words, but the frustration was palpable. The reason? The in-flight Internet was not working. He had planned to watch a movie, but that was not to be.

His irritation reminded me of how easily and rapidly we revise expectations. Until very recently, surfing the web at cruising altitude would have been considered too fanciful. Now its absence was enough to discount all the good. He forgot that he was physically comfortable, the flight was on time, he was sipping the beverage of his choice, and many other aspects had gone right that day.

I don't blame him. This is just the way the human mind works—programmed to be dissatisfied. In this default state, we bypass contentment and thus happiness. This is normal. Normal, however, isn't optimal. We should take charge of our minds and train ourselves to be content if we (and our loved ones) are safe, are not in pain, have food, and feel loved (by at least one person). Everything else is a bonus.

How do we find such contentment? I find statements that "contentment only comes from within" incomplete. The external world sets the conditions for us to feel content. Abject poverty, imminent danger, emotional abusers, or severe pain—none of these is conducive to contentment. Anxious or depressed minds, or those that are delusional, paranoid, or hate-filled, can't be content either.

Contentment comes when the external reality matches our inner expectations. In the modern world, we have some control over both. A good pursuit simultaneously enables deeper appreciation of reality and lowers the expectations, so one feels content while continuing to progress.

Such contentment isn't meant to imply apathy or lower standards. It is meant to say, I am enough, and I have enough. I will savor what I have and who I am, as I continue to expand what I have and who I am.

What happens once you achieve such contentment? In addition to helping you be happier, kinder, and more effective, your contentment, curiously, gives way to a state of discontent—you're no longer content with your own happiness; you start caring about many others. You become passionate to decrease the world's suffering and relieve pain. You no longer seek eternal peace for yourself. Instead, you strive to fill your life with meaning to help others find peace.

A passionate state of discontent geared to fulfill an altruistic meaning is more desirable than blissful contentment from personal success and comfort. In that mixed state of feeling personally fulfilled but discontented with the problems of the world, you'll discover the greatest happiness.

May you find contentment; may your contentment power your passions.

Take care.

Amit

* Suggested practice: Today, I will work, assuming I am helping people who I really care about.
(For additional practices, visit Stressfree.org/Immerse/)

70. Wiser Choices

Give your best and don't dwell on the outcome.

Dear friend,

My four-year-old can't lift a table or push a heavy chair. Yet she wants to be admired as a strong, independent "big girl." We often help out—as she pushes the chair, we add our force, while making sure she doesn't see that we are doing so. With the mission accomplished, we all celebrate her success. I know when her innocence fades she will figure out this ruse. Hopefully by that time her biceps will have the strength to open the car doors and push heavier chairs.

I am increasingly realizing that my accomplishments aren't too dissimilar. I can influence my effort and intention. My effort and intention, however, are only a small part of the equation. Countless external forces, known and unknown, and the play of probability collude with each other and my efforts to determine the outcome. In my hand are my diligence and good intentions. The rest is a large unknown that I can only imagine and observe.

Internalizing this reality helps me stop obsessing about the outcomes. I realize that I shouldn't peg my self-esteem on the results, unpredictable as they are. Instead, I should focus on effort and intentions. I hope to keep striving without tiring and to fulfill a meaning without experiencing burnout.

I should also recognize that I only fail when I don't try. If I give a good try, no matter the outcome, I can't fail.

A good attempt entails a tension among choices. Choosing one equals letting go of another. Choosing isn't easy because letting go isn't easy. My mind wants the benefit of both choices while committing effort to only one (sometimes none!). I am amused by my mind's irrational greed.

Once I choose, I should chase my choice and give it my best—I should focus, sweat, persevere, and go the extra mile, with patience and creativity. However, once the dice are cast, I should leave them to chance. My effort is a small wave in the ocean of events that influence an outcome. I believe if my intentions are pure, my wave will be in sync with the tide. Chance might choose to favor me.

So I should choose (not drift), chase (not be lax), keep good intentions, and then leave the outcome to chance.

May the tide favor your little wave of good intention; may your goodness create a new wave if the tide changes its direction.

Take care.

Amit

* Suggested practice: Today, I will focus my attention on my efforts and intentions, not the outcome.
  (For additional practices, visit Stressfree.org/Immerse/)

Week 36

*D*uring this week you'll develop a healthy attitude toward your assets, and you'll live your days as a student, fully willing to learn.

71. Your Lease

Your possessions are temporarily leased to you.

Dear friend,

When I depart an aircraft after a flight, I often notice eager passengers waiting to board the same plane that I just exited. The seat I occupied didn't belong to me; I leased it for a short while. The home I live in, my office space, even the molecules that constitute my body will be with me for a small, finite time. So will money.

Money has been around us for at least four thousand years, if not longer (as early as 9,000 BC, cattle and grain were used as money). We use our 240 trillion dollars (the approximate combined net worth of all the households on our planet) to acquire goods, get services, or pay down debt. Money is thus very important, but beyond a threshold, it is very ineffective in providing lasting peace and happiness.

This is because as we acquire money, our wants and threshold for happiness both rise. Further, when we have more, we fear losing it and get busy with protecting it. Money thus by itself can't provide sustained happiness. Asking money to deliver lasting happiness is like asking my boom box to play a 3D movie. It won't happen.

Two perspectives might help you get more joy out of that dollar. One, money is an enabler; it is the means, not the end. Money helps you access the two core sources of lasting happiness—meaningful connection and creative pursuits. Caring and kind connections, in which you accept the other people as they are, make up one of our core sources of happiness. Similarly, creative pursuits, particularly the meaningful ones, where we lose our sense of self in a state of flow, are immensely pleasing. You need some money to experience both connection and creativity.

The second perspective involves seeing yourself as a conduit for the flow of energy between its source and the receivers. The source can choose the amount of energy it is willing to pass through you. The energy doesn't belong to you, but for the moment it pauses in your coffers, you're responsible for being its good steward.

This attitude will allow you to use the fleeting money to buy timeless happiness (through connection and creative pursuits), keep equanimity amid losses and gains, and experience a measure of financial freedom. It'll help you see money as a transient source of energy. If you try to grab or hoard it with purely selfish intent, it might not serve you as you had hoped. However, if you use it to fulfill a prosocial meaning, such as helping others acquire life's essentials, you might convert the transient energy into enduring memories of fulfilling experiences, compassionate actions, and grateful moments. That, I believe, would be a good investment.

May you never struggle to acquire life's essentials; may you help others acquire life's essentials.

Take care.

Amit

* Suggested practice: Today, I will spend extra time with my loved ones and friends and be fully attentive, knowing I have only a limited time with them.
(For additional practices, visit Stressfree.org/Immerse/)

72. The Best Job in the World

What is the best job in the world?

Dear friend,

Each breath is precious. An individual breath, however, can sustain you only for a few seconds. To be alive, you have to keep breathing. The same is true about knowledge. You may have learned all your life, but you will need to keep learning to continue to use what you already know. Thus, if you wish to be successful, creative, and happy, you'll have to embrace the ultimate job, from which you can never retire—that of being a student.

A person who is learning and is enrolled in an educational institution is defined as a student. A good student is open to critique and isn't fearful of being proven wrong. That openness keeps the student young and fresh each day. It also keeps him or her humble.

I believe the best job in the world is that of being a student. Even if you have graduated top of the class, continue to embrace the job of being a student, which will stay with you the rest of your life. No matter what you do, always choose to remain a student.

Once you feel you have graduated and are now in a "real" job (and thus no longer a formal student), you risk losing curiosity and, with that, joy. Research shows the majority of current workers (up to three-quarters) do not enjoy their work. Two out of three workers report work as their top stressor. With an average worker spending forty-seven hours each week at work (America is the most worked country in the industrialized world), no wonder we are also the most anxious nation.

Workplace stress, because of demand-resource imbalance and loss of curiosity, joy, control, and meaning, is forcing a high proportion of people to contemplate premature retirement. For example, a full 80 percent of senior physicians employed in the British NHS are thinking of early retirement. That's a loss of precious experience and wisdom collected over generations.

While several efforts to help professionals are being implemented at the institutional and national level, you can do a lot on your own. At an individual level, we can work to overcome our stress by trying to match demand with resources, control the controllable, find greater meaning in work, and reinvigorate the sense of curiosity and joy we had when we started working (i.e., become a student again).

If you have already graduated, even from a master's or PhD course, reenroll as a freshman in the college of life. Like it or not, you will always remain a freshman on this giant college campus called earth, with life as your professor. That's not a bad thing. It'll keep you humble and open to new experiences. That is one of the best ways to continue to grow, succeed, avoid letting success get to your head, or keep a high workload from pushing you into burnout.

May you wake up each day a little less ignorant than the previous day.

Take care.

Amit

* Suggested practice: Today, I will consider everyone around me as my teacher.
(For additional practices, visit Stressfree.org/Immerse/)

Week 37

During this week you'll sidestep your ingrained biases so you can more easily access the truth, and you'll renew your commitment to living a life of integrity.

73. Truth and Temptations

Your version of truth is colored by your mind's ignorance and the unfulfilled desires that create biases.

Dear friend,

Truth is sacred; it transcends time and isn't limited by epochs or paradigms. Wisdom comes in knowing, internalizing, and living by the truth. The perception of the truth, however, varies depending on one's state of mind and present motives. The ultimate truth for squirrels might lie in knowing the facts that lead them to the nuts; for dogs, truth is in the smells, and for an eagle, in discovering the slightest change in patterns that can take her to the prey. Truth, when looked at with limited lenses, becomes limited.

When I am hungry, because of biological hunger or from pure temptations, my version of truth is limited. An old expression I heard says that for a very hungry person, two plus two isn't four—it is four pieces of bread. A hungry person searches for food in the world. In other words, I see the truth colored by my biases.

Biases are preconceived beliefs based on incomplete information. They are often guided by personal preference. Every aspect of life where individual opinions come into play, be it science, politics, economics, marketing, or sports, has biases.

Biases do not always reflect dishonesty or intentional wrongdoing. They reflect our four core inabilities—the inability of the human mind to integrate all the important variables, the inability to allocate appropriate weight to the considered variables, the inability to recognize personal limitations, and the inability to separate personal beliefs from personal preferences. Thousands of biases have been described in multiple disciplines. Racism, sexism, and classism are three classical biases that play out in society.

A crucial step to start seeing the truth is to remove personal preferences. Recognize that personal preferences aren't easy to remove, because while my biological desires are few, the desires of my mind are unquenchable. Unless I put a lid on my mind, the truth I see will be limited.

The next important step is to recognize my own limitations. I must accept that my mind might never be completely free of temptations, and hence I may never be able to see the complete truth bereft of any bias. Further, my brain has limited working memory (the equivalent of a computer's RAM), and that limits my ability to perceive the full depth and breadth in any experience. I should try to free myself of my predispositions and be willing to listen and learn. That is my only hope to get closer to the reality.

As I work on myself, I hope the truth also finds me worthy and seeks me, for my days are finite and progress slower than desired.

May you seek the truth; may the truth seek you.

Take care.

Amit

*   Suggested practice: Today, I will exercise self-control with at least one temptation.
(For additional practices, visit Stressfree.org/Immerse/)

74. *Honesty*

Be extraordinarily grateful today if you don't have to be dishonest for bare survival.

Dear friend,

Honesty means speaking and living by the truth. With respect to honesty, people come in four different flavors. Some are habitually dishonest. Others choose to be honest as long as it serves their purpose. Still others are, barring extreme situations, committed to honesty, no matter whether it hurts or harms them. The fourth type of honesty is dumb or cruel honesty. If you know that your honesty is likely to start World War III or cause suffering for millions, then it might be best to keep your mouth shut.

The world is tired of habitual dishonesty. It doesn't need dumb or cruel honesty either. Fortunately, both of these are rare. Most of us fit into the second or the third pattern, where we are honest as long as it serves our purpose or remain committed to honesty barring extreme situations.

Quite often, we shift between the second and third types depending on life's happenings and the influence of role models. Consider yourself lucky today if you aren't forced into dishonest thoughts, words, or actions. For example, imagine your child is crying from intense hunger and you can only get food by lying to someone. What would you do? Most likely you'd lie, wouldn't you? I certainly would.

I have judged others for their dishonesty, not knowing their constraints. I shouldn't judge that way. I should recognize that I can be honest today only because I am not challenged so. If I were placed in their precarious situation, I would likely slip. The intention, however, varies, and beyond a limit, it gets subjective. In the above example, if my two kids were crying from hunger and I hoarded food for twenty children just to be safe, despite knowing that the supplies were limited, then I am being dishonest.

Every twenty-four-karat-gold ornament is impure, because pure gold is too soft to become an ornament. So are we. The worthwhile impurity within us is that of altruistic dishonesty. When you are willing to let go of personal salvation for the larger good by not speaking a brutally honest and harmful truth, you are doing the righteous thing. Dishonesty, however, needs very careful judgment and utter selflessness.

Every day my circumstances do not force me to be dishonest is a day to be deeply grateful. I should not judge others if I find them dishonest until I know the details of what prompted them to act. I should also not gloat about my honesty. My honesty is a privilege, and I am deeply grateful for it.

May you never run into a situation where you are forced to be dishonest; may you not prematurely judge those you find dishonest.

Take care.

Amit

* Suggested practice: Today, I will live my day with my deepest values to serve a higher meaning.
(For additional practices, visit Stressfree.org/Immerse/)

Week 38

*D*uring this week you'll actively look for goodness and truth around you, and you'll more fully appreciate your world by softening your desire for perfection.

75. Light and Darkness

The wider I open my eyes, the more light I can see.

Dear friend,

Vultures soar in the sky, looking for carcass, while humming birds dart from one tree to the next, looking for fresh blossoms. They both work hard and find what they are looking for. We find what we seek.

Our choices influence our future. We can direct our life with four different kinds of seeking—seeking the truth, seeking the positive, seeking the negative, or nonseeking.

The ideal seeking, I believe, is to seek the truth. Truth, however, needs sharp, discerning eyes, and a deep, discerning mind, for truth often hides amid noise, and it can be rather unpleasant and unnerving. A mind that can assimilate the truth needs the power of equanimity. Equanimity isn't for the faint of heart, given our proclivity for strong preferences. An interim solution allows one to see the truth in its most optimistic version.

Next in order is to seek the positive. Seeking the positive helps you find the good within the bad and the phenomenal within the trivial. Positivity, however, if out of balance, risks unbridled, unrealistic optimism and delayed disengagement from a difficult situation. I have seen many abusive relationships in which the abused partner lingered by constantly reframing the situation as not that bad and likely to get better. (My personal rule is to take the exit if someone twice does something to me that I would never do to that person.)

Next is seeking the negative. Seeking negativity biases you to find the bad within the good. You stop taking chances. Your daily guiding principle becomes, "better safe than sorry." Forever looking out for the bad, you isolate yourself and spend most of your days inside your head—paranoid, fearful, and in the prey mode.

Nonseeking is the fourth option. Nonseeking, I believe, is mostly a theoretical ideal. Remaining completely open to experience with no preferences may be feasible if you live alone, have no dependents, and have few if any worries in the world. For most practical purposes, it may feel good to read about such hermitic existence in wellness magazines, but it is difficult if not impossible to emulate.

I believe living a life combining the first three types of seeking offers an optimal mix. Seek the truth about the self and the nature of life; seek the good in your partner, friends, and loved ones; and seek the negative in lost opportunities and past regrets so you can reframe them.

Such intentionality in your seeking influences your receptivity, which in turn affects your experience. For example, your perception of sweetness depends not only on the inherent sweetness of the food but also on the sensitivity of your taste receptors. After you suck on a very sweet candy, an otherwise sweet pear will taste bland; the same pear might taste particularly sweet after a hot soup or a slice of pizza. Your taste receptors that carry the sweet message, after they have tasted the candy, no longer respond to the pear with the same enthusiasm.

Extrapolating to the totality of life, no moment is totally dark. Light is always present. The brightness depends on how wide my eyes are open. Even through the darkest moments, when I look back I can find some light that was not visible to me during those moments. In the future I should keep this faith—that it never gets totally dark; if I make the effort to open my eyes just a little wider, they'll see the light.

I suspect the light itself seeks the eyes that are searching. For just as the light fulfills the purpose of the eyes, the eyes fulfill the purpose of the light. You're precious.

May you seek the light; may the light seek you.

Take care.

Amit

* Suggested practice: Today, I will more fully appreciate every person I interact with, assuming they all are trying to do their best. (For additional practices, visit Stressfree.org/Immerse/)

76. Fully Alive

Be willing to improve, and soften your urge to improve others.

Dear friend,

After a full meal, I often find myself in front of the refrigerator, wondering what more I could eat. My one-quart stomach may have no space left, but my mind isn't satisfied. This is because, even though I ate enough calories, I was not present to experience them. My still-hungry mind doesn't like the idea of the meal being over. Life is a bit like that.

I am not fully alive when I am not present for my moments. I am not truly present when I am locked in a wandering mind, or when I want the present experience to be something other than it is. When I get busy with what comes next, I bypass what's happening now. I invest most of my conscious moments in trying to improve a future conscious moment.

With spending the bulk of my days this way, I realize I really didn't savor my morsels of life. I fear I'll be forced to leave the table too soon, dissatisfied, unaccomplished, and unwilling to leave.

Why do I do that? Why do I spend most of my moments thinking about another moment? My brain has acquired a hobby of spending time with itself. My brain is tremendously skillful at generating an endless dialogue inside my head. This dialogue is a soup of gossips, imaginations, fears, fantasies, regrets, plans, and so much more. The flavor changes, albeit slightly, from one day to the next; that keeps the internal conversation interesting and on autopilot.

With a full trilogy playing inside my head, I perceive the outside world as boring, and not particularly novel or pleasing. Gradually, my brain sculpts multilane highways that host the inner dialogue, trapping my attention. Eventually, this mind wandering becomes an effortless habit, like brushing teeth in the morning. Unlike brushing teeth, however, this habit crowds most of my awake moments. It becomes as ingrained as breathing.

How do I break this habit? One idea is to weaken the allure of my mind's content.

My mind works extra shifts to expand my version of self and guard my physical and emotional safety. Between physical and emotional safety, I spend the bulk of my time guarding my emotional vulnerabilities. If I could be willing to be a little more emotionally vulnerable than I currently am, and if I could temporarily soften my expectation of perfection, then I would more easily inhabit the passing moments. Then I would find I had lived a full life and wouldn't fear leaving the table (world) too soon. Curiously, this might help me live longer and be healthier. At least that's what the science says.

May you not seek perfection or invulnerability, and through this non-seeking, may you become a little more perfect and a little less vulnerable.

Take care.

Amit

* Suggested practice: Today, I will spend at least five minutes consciously choosing not to plan, problem solve, or worry.
(For additional practices, visit Stressfree.org/Immerse/)

Week 39

During this week you'll embrace the essence of philosophy, poetry, and spirituality—compassion, and you'll become stronger by aligning your life with your deepest values.

77. The Ultimate Philosophy

The ultimate language of love is compassion.

Dear friend,

Love means wanting good for the other. Love is the biological equivalent of gravity. It provides the meaning that glues relationships together. It comes in many flavors—that of playmate (*ludus*), friend or family (*philia*), partner (*pragma*), self (*philautia*), and the whole world (*agape*). There is also the purely physical attraction, often called *eros*.

Love often starts with infatuation, which turns into passion. Passion leads to commitment, which spawns nurturing. Nurturing naturally transforms into selfless life-long devotion to the beloved. Passion, commitment, nurturing, and devotion are all powered and enabled by a common single force—kindness.

World over, the single most desirable attribute in a person is kindness. Your daily kindness is an expression of the most vital and most powerful force—compassion, the ultimate wisdom and the ultimate love.

Compassion wants good for the other. Love and compassion are thus the same. Compassion recognizes and validates pain, and intends and strives to relieve it. Compassion is happy in others' happiness, with no occasion for envy. Compassion is the essence of emotional intelligence, professionalism, leadership, and morality.

I haven't met anyone who is compassionate yet incompetent. Compassionate people naturally care, and thus they work diligently to acquire the skills to help and serve. Any business entity that embraces compassion will eventually outshine its competition. Health care is using knowledge and technology to deliver compassion. Remove compassion, and you are left only with disease management.

Compassion is the primary virtue that creates a livable and happy world. You are the parents' enemy if you intend to hurt their children. You are the enemy of the creation if you hurt the creation's children—all of us. I love those who love my children; I believe the entire creation will love us if we love creation's children—by feeling and expressing compassion to each other.

When you remove the juice from an orange, the remaining fiber is tasteless and bereft of nutrients. It loses its "orangeness." Similarly, if you remove compassion from life, every philosophy and belief will become dry. Compassion is the vital essence and the primal force that keeps human life humming on our planet.

If you wish to keep our planet alive, practice compassion. If you wish to receive kindness, give kindness. That's the timeless commandment.

May you and the little ones you care about thrive in a world built with compassion; may you help others and their little ones thrive in a world you build with compassion.

Take care.

Amit

* Suggested practice: Today, I will be extra kind and patient with every person, familiar or stranger.
(For additional practices, visit Stressfree.org/Immerse/)

78. Your Strength

You derive strength and courage from the values you protect.

Dear friend,

The subtle is stronger than the gross. The visible forces of nature (tides, hurricanes, and volcanoes) are dwarfed by the subtle, invisible powers of nature (gravity, nuclear forces, and magnetism).

The visible forces of the mind (hatred, envy, revenge, and anger) are extremely weak in front of the quiet but infinitely stronger powers (gratitude, compassion, acceptance, and forgiveness).

Your greatest strength lies in harnessing and aligning with the stronger forces. While in the very short term, revenge may seem stronger, in the long term, it is forgiveness that will give you greater strength. Uncontrolled anger may look like pure adrenaline, but it is compassion that unlocks the greatest energy. Often, I can't see this because my vision is foggy, my longevity short, and my wisdom limited.

You will face setbacks on the righteous path and will need constancy of effort powered by courage. Courage doesn't decimate fear; courage acts despite the fear. The courage that David showed against Goliath and the cowardly lion against the Wicked Witch (in *The Wizard of Oz*) has sound scientific underpinning. Research shows fear is hosted by almond-shaped nuclei in the brain called the amygdala. Courage activates the brain's anterior cingulate cortex, which mentors and quiets the amygdala activity. Complete lack of fear isn't desirable, as any parent of a two-year-old can tell you. Total fearlessness is actually pathological; it risks putting you in harm's way. Further, we find great joy and growth in overcoming fears, not in not having fears.

How does one find such courage? I have talked to thousands of folks about courageous people in their personal lives, asking them what they thought provided the courage. Three themes have emerged. Courageous people are often other-centric, finding great meaning in helping their fellow beings; they have good role models whose principles they imbibe; and many find great courage from their faith. A combination of these paths helps such people lead lives driven by passion and meaning rather than fear. These three themes are connected by the single principle that most people with an abundance of courage live by higher values. The values they protect power their courage.

The values of compassion and forgiveness, higher meaning and selflessness, patience and contentment, are timeless and powerful. They provide strength to anyone who lives to protect them. These values can't be destroyed. If you become their temporary custodian, you become indestructible in the process.

May you feel strong and brave because of the values you protect.

Take care.

Amit

* Suggested practice: Today, I will feel stronger, protected by my values. (For additional practices, visit Stressfree.org/Immerse/)

Week 40

During this week you'll see others as sacred and priceless and feel connected with everyone working to decrease global suffering.

79. Deeper Vision

See others from a deeper place within you.

Dear friend,

I ask an audience of over nine hundred people, "How many of you know someone in your life who is priceless to you?" Every single hand goes up. The chances are all of you can think of someone who is infinitely precious to you. You are also infinitely precious to someone. But that's not how we look at each other. Why?

It is because we have limited instruments—both our sensory organs and our minds. Let's first talk about our sensory organs.

Our eyes are phenomenal, yet they have several limitations. Our eyes adapt well to the dark, but below a threshold, the light photons, even if they induce a chemical reaction on the retina, don't create a neural response. We can only see a narrow spectrum of light that ranges from 380 to 720 nanometers. We have blind spots and are blind to our blind spots. Our eyes can't see anything behind our heads. Further, when you scan the horizon on a flat savannah, you can't see beyond 3.1 miles, because the earth's surface curves out at that point.

Our other senses are also fabulous but limited. We have a narrow range of hearing, both in terms of intensity and frequency. We can't hear all the sounds our puppies or dolphins can. Our noses are a million times less sensitive than those of dogs. Our taste buds, at least in research studies, can't tell the difference between red wine and white wine.

Like our senses, our minds are also phenomenal yet limited. Our minds are restless and irrational. We are biased and unaware of our biases, and we often make quick (and incorrect) decisions based on limited information. We can't integrate the total picture, and we are poor at using simple mathematical and statistical principles in our daily lives.

With those limits to my senses and mind, I see people around me very superficially. I see them as a means to an end. I don't see them in their circle of love, and I truly struggle with finding the sacred in the annoying. I am a work in progress.

If I could see further into the future, I would recognize the transience of the mighty, the preciousness and power of the subtle, and the indestructibility of the virtues. The virtues transcend time. People a thousand generations younger than us will rediscover and find peace through gratitude, compassion, and forgiveness, just as people a thousand generations prior to us did. I will also see the circle of love that surrounds each person.

I shouldn't allow my eyes and my mind to set the limits for what I can see. I should see others from the deepest place within me. Once I do that, I will see each person surrounded by a garland of loved ones. I will see each one of us as a sacred, priceless being, and not just a transient blob of condensed energy. Such sight will make me and the world around me kinder and happier.

May you see the depths, deeper than your eyes can show; may such vision help you see others as sacred and priceless beings.

Take care.

Amit

* Suggested practice: Today, I will try not to place people in my precast molds.
(For additional practices, visit Stressfree.org/Immerse/)

80. Global Enemy

Our common global enemy is collective human suffering.

Dear friend,

As I write these thoughts, I am recovering from a scathing one-star review of my previous book. Last night when I held my four-year-old close in my lap, she provided sobering feedback: "Daddy, your teeth are so yellow!" My most recent talk wasn't as well received as I had expected. I could use a little pat on the back at this moment.

I don't have a secure sense of myself. My concept of self depends on my perception of how others perceive me. I get inflated or deflated depending on the amount of air the world pumps into my ego balloon. I am biased to perceive the most recent and most negative feedback as the most potent. My relationship with the self is thus ever changing, and that colors and tracks my relationship with others.

This dynamicity makes life interesting, but it saps tremendous energy. The grazing cattle of negative perceptions rapidly devour the tiny sapling of connection that I develop with people. I am thus unable to form strong roots that could feed the stem, branches, and leaves of a community around me. In this state, my life becomes barren and lonely.

I need to shed the habit of constantly reevaluating relationships. I shouldn't anchor my relationships in biased perceptions, flimsy and superficial as they often are. I should anchor my connections in deeper meaning.

The meaning found in collective gains or success can unite us. But such meaning is vulnerable, because the much-sought-after gains that defined me yesterday stop being meaningful once acquired. The gains can also be lost in the blink of an eye. I have read or heard about people losing billions of dollars in a day and about stellar reputations built over a lifetime melting with one imprudent tweet. I need to look elsewhere for a secure meaning.

I believe the one meaning that can bring us all together, which will never pale, is the collective meaning of decreasing suffering. You and I can join in an effort to minimize suffering and maximize happiness for our planet's children. That is our primary evolutionary responsibility. Relationships developed to serve such a meaning will be invulnerable to minor disagreements and negative perceptions.

The first step to decrease suffering is to recognize it in others. When you are stuck in your pain and I am stuck in mine, we are trapped in our pain. But when you look at my pain and I look at yours, with an intention to soothe, then even though we are still looking at pain, we heal rather than hurt.

Let's join in to serve the common goal of eradicating suffering. Therein lies the hope of us working and walking together for the rest of our lives.

May a circle of love surround you; may the thread of a common meaning hold this circle together.

Take care.

Amit

* Suggested practice: Today, I will think less about my own struggles and instead focus on all that has gone right in my life.
(For additional practices, visit Stressfree.org/Immerse/)

Week 41

*D*uring this week you'll recognize that despite superficial differences everyone has struggles similar to yours, and you'll learn how the tooth fairy's visits could have different meanings depending on how old you are.

81. Knowing Others

Others are more similar to you than you think.

Dear friend,

A typical supermarket has about forty thousand items on the shelf. Given that an average person samples less than 1 percent of these items in a year, you likely aren't aware of 99 percent of the items in your supermarket.

Even the items I purchase and use are barely familiar to me. When I see a bottle of shampoo or jar of pickles, I only know what the label shows (which I seldom read). Each of these items has a unique journey from start to finish that isn't known to me. I know these objects only from the middle—neither the beginning nor the end.

Similarly, I don't know any person in the world from the beginning to the end. Everyone I am familiar with, I know from the middle. I don't know where you were before you magically showed up on this planet or in what worlds your future awaits. I know your idiosyncrasies, but I don't know your constraints.

If I find you unreasonable, very likely I am missing a critical detail. Perhaps you are justified from within your perspective. Perhaps we both would be better off if we could have a heart-to-heart chat. Very likely, however, that won't happen. You feel most comfortable in your shell, just as I do in mine. I don't know how you'd perceive me if I laid it all bare. You don't know that either. So we drag through life—judging, feeling judged, wishing we could again receive the unconditional love that we experienced when we were little, when someone made sure we ate enough fruits and veggies, and celebrated every single burp of ours.

While we will never know each other's complete story, we can assume it isn't very different. You have struggles and dreams similar to mine. You strive to keep your world safe and fed, as I do. We both want to do the right thing, but sometimes we aren't sure what the right thing is. We commit silly mistakes; we forget and can't easily forgive.

I think I know you better than I thought. Through knowing you I know myself better than I did. I wish to keep trying to know you and myself, because once we know each other, I am confident we will each drop our weapons. You'll get busy healing my hurts, and I will get busy healing yours. The world will be better for it.

May you see your own reflection in the world and, through discovering that similarity, default to kindness and generosity.

Take care.

Amit

* Suggested practice: Today, I will send a silent good wish to everyone I see, knowing everyone is struggling.
(For additional practices, visit Stressfree.org/Immerse/)

82. Tooth Fairy

If you assign a positive meaning to a loss, the loss could become a gain.

Dear friend,

I remember the gleam in my elder daughter's eyes when she (finally) discovered her first loose tooth. She looked forward to the visit from the tooth fairy. The tooth fairy, she had heard, was magical and kind, and she left interesting notes and of course, brought money. In fact, not having a single loose tooth, when every child around you is gloriously shedding teeth, can be very stressful for a six-year-old.

In a survey of children who had become aware of the unreality of the tooth fairy, a full 75 percent reported liking the custom. I believe tooth fairies across the world have given kids more joy than most real-life characters have.

Fast-forward fifty years. How do you feel about the tooth fairy visiting you at age sixty? We spend all our life brushing and flossing to prevent that from happening, and when it does, we spend money and tolerate pain to fix it.

The difference between the two experiences is the meaning. A loose tooth at age five means we are growing and conforming to the expected norm. A fresh tooth is also waiting in the wings. A loose tooth at age sixty reflects the failure of our efforts. It reminds us that we are getting older and are finite.

As intelligent beings, we have a choice. Recognizing that the same loss could bring different emotions that depend not on the loss itself but on its meaning, what if we could change the meaning of our losses? What if loose and lost teeth could reflect the arrival of wisdom? What if we could be grateful that the tooth served us for all these years, that we have many more teeth that continue to serve us, and that much better care is available now to preserve the remaining teeth? What if we could see a lost tooth as a reminder to take better care of ourselves? What if we also could be more compassionate toward those who do not have the privilege of good dental care or who have a medical condition that causes premature tooth loss?

If we cultivate that attitude, we might transform our loss into a gain—that of wisdom. Perhaps that's the meaning of losses. A loss or gain is a judgment based on the meaning you assign to an experience. Both losses and gains help us obtain wisdom.

May you have more gains than losses; may you develop wisdom through both gains and losses.

Take care.

Amit

*   Suggested practice: Today, I will think of at least one way my loss may have helped me.
    (For additional practices, visit Stressfree.org/Immerse/)

Week 42

During this week you'll discover how to see the light in others, and you will honor the similarities and differences you have with others.

83. Who Are You?

Seeing the light in others will help you see the light within yourself.

Dear friend,

"Who am I?" is a powerful question. Spiritual luminaries have held the thread of this question and tracked inward to attain profound insights. While doing so, some have arrived at the perception of emptiness, while others have found oneness, a connection to everything as a unified whole.

I struggle with finding meaning in emptiness. Emptiness could calm me, but it disconnects me from the world that I find solid and real.

Experience of oneness, an intensely pleasant feeling, is more tangible. However, whether this feeling of oneness is truly an enlightened state or a mere sensory phenomenon produced by the firing of specific brain networks isn't clear. Scientists note that people experiencing certain strokes and brain tumors sometimes have a similar perception of oneness. The activation (or inhibition) of certain brain areas can provide similar experiences of unity. I don't find it worthy to commit my life to evoking just a brain state, however pleasing it might be.

To me, seeing the light in others, by becoming a kinder human being, is more important than the sensory experience of seeing the light within me. The question that I believe directly leads me to kindness isn't, "Who am I?" It is, "Who are you?"

That question prompts me to look deeper. I see profoundness unseen before. I stop seeing you as a means to an end. I see you as a conscious, sentient being with the same struggles as mine. I see you in your circle of love. I see the sacred in you. I identify with the "I" in you.

My commitment to seeing you at greater depths makes me kinder. I believe that through practicing kindness for you, I will become kind to myself. In the process, I will live a good life.

The ultimate wisdom one attains after a lifetime of learning teaches one to become a kinder human being. Why not start right there as a first step?

Thank you for being you.

May you seek kindness before oneness, meaning before fulfillment, and compassion before salvation.

Take care.

Amit

*   Suggested practice: Today, I will assume each person is helping me in profound ways.
(For additional practices, visit Stressfree.org/Immerse/)

84. Changing and Changeless

Let the changing be perceived as novel and not overwhelming; let the changeless be perceived as comforting and not boring.

Dear friend,

The idea that created you and me hasn't changed. That same idea put hearts and lungs in our chests, brains in our skulls, and intestines, livers, and kidneys below our diaphragms. I was born with and still have this basic design. My eyes, which look at the world, are the same eyes I had the day I was born, and the person behind the eyes, the one that perceives the world, is the same. All these are changeless.

But there is another part that always changes. Each moment, my thoughts change, my breath changes, even my heart rhythm shows subtle changes from one beat to another. (Within limits, the greater this beat-to-beat variation, the healthier the heart.) My physical body thus remains in a constant flux; no structure in my physical body in its present form is precisely as it was when I was born.

Further, each of the fifty to seventy-five trillion cells in my physical body has its own natural trajectory. The cells that line the intestines live for only a few days; the skin cells live for a few weeks, while the red blood cells stay in circulation for about four months. Every year 1 percent of my heart muscles are created afresh. I am like a river—flowing, ever moving.

The changing parts of you and me differ from each other, even if the differences are too subtle to be recognized by the naked eye or a fancy microscope. The changeless part of you and me are shared. My default is to create separations when I look at differences and get bored with the similarities. I should choose otherwise.

I should focus on the changing part of you to value your uniqueness and the shared part of ours to connect with our commonness. The changing and the changeless complete each other. Without the changing, the world wouldn't have moved beyond its primordial soup; without the changeless, the world wouldn't have a firm anchor to manifest life. The changeless is the screen; the changing is the movie that plays on it. Both feed each other.

Value the changing (the differences) in those in front of you and love the changeless (the commonalities) in all.

May the changing within you honor and value the changing in others; may the changeless within you love the changeless in all.

Take care.

Amit

*   Suggested practice: Today, I will be extra compassionate toward those who, because they are perceived as different, get mistreated. (For additional practices, visit Stressfree.org/Immerse/)

Week 43

*D*uring this week you'll decrease your vulnerability by deepening your connection with values and softening your attachment to cravings and fears, and you'll feed your whole being—body, mind, and soul.

85. Varying Vulnerabilities

As long as we have cravings and fears, although the specific vulnerabilities might change, we will stay vulnerable.

Dear friend,

There was a time I couldn't tolerate hunger. I am told I would wail at the top of my lungs when hungry. As I grew older, winning in Chutes and Ladders became a big deal, followed by pushing the elevator buttons. Everything I wanted, I had to have, right at that moment.

My wholeness depended on all kinds of little things—holding a piece of rock, pushing random buttons, watching my favorite TV show, coloring with crayons. I was very vulnerable.

I still am vulnerable, but the details have changed. I no longer care about crayons. I do care about academic success. I want everyone to like me. I want to be in people's good books, to be talked up in gossip. I want people to remember me. I want to create a legacy.

I have given the keys to my mind's kingdom to many others. That makes me vulnerable. My vulnerabilities depend on what I find meaningful, particularly in the material domain.

I need to change my sense of self. Instead of protecting my desires and fears, I should protect my conscience. I should expand my kindness. I should develop causeless gratitude. My meaning shouldn't be contingent on defeating others. Instead, I should value inspiring others. I should remind others how good they are.

I have realized that I can't get rid of my cravings, fears, and selfishness. I can, however, cultivate a healthy attitude toward these predispositions. I can cultivate a craving to help as many as I can. I can nurture the fear of living a meaningless life. I can try to enhance the self by connecting my thoughts, words, and actions with a higher meaning.

I believe this expanded meaning will decrease my vulnerability. With this meaning I will step out of competition with the world. I will escape the prison of short-term gratifications. The previous cravings and fears that enslaved me won't be replaced by new ones. I will experience freedom. I will be happy and help others find greater happiness.

May you swap your fears, cravings, and selfishness for gratitude, compassion, and selflessness.

Take care.

Amit

*   Suggested practice: Today, I will not fulfill any desire that goes against my values.
(For additional practices, visit Stressfree.org/Immerse/)

86. The Sacred Food

Each day feed your body, mind, and soul.

Dear friend,

Modern aircraft seating comes in multiple varieties. Some of the variations in seating include different types of phone slots, USB and AC ports, tablet ledges, back pitches, winged headrests, fold-down tables, leg and arm rests, recliners, fully flat beds, all the way to large private rooms and seat-bed suites. On an international flight, as I sat with stiff, cramping legs on a middle seat in economy class, I wondered about the comforts of the world business class. I surmised that once I got that upgrade, after a few flights, I would start wondering about a chartered flight. Next I might desire a Learjet, or even a fleet of them. Soon thereafter, I might want to own an island. Then I might worry about how to sustain this lifestyle, concerned that a competitor's product might decrease my company's revenue stream, potentially decreasing the stock price and thus the value of my options, which I would have used as collateral to fund my extravaganza.

This treadmill occurs because I have forgotten who I am and what I am really hungry for. As I look deeply, I realize I don't have one hunger; I have five of them—namely food-hunger, ego-hunger, emotional-hunger, creativity-hunger, and meaning-hunger.

The material food satisfies my food-hunger with nutrition. Nutrition, however, isn't just calories and taste. The fragrance, the color, the sound, the touch, and the love that has been poured into the food, all add to its nutrition. The more I make eating a multisensory experience, the greater contentment I find in it and the lesser my need to gorge on extra calories.

Ego-hunger spurs me to chase material wealth and fame. It tickles me to acquire things. The things please because of their innate value, and even more so, because of their novelty. We are designed to seek new and fresh objects and experiences. If the things themselves had phenomenal value, we would never get tired of them. But we do. Hence, the things aren't the real thing. They are a side helping. The main course is what feeds the higher three hungers.

Emotional-hunger seeks love, expressed as kindness, appreciation, acceptance, connection, caring, attention, trust, respect, intimacy, and more. We have at least four different compartments of emotional-hunger—with partners, close loved ones, professional connections, and friends and others. Rejection in any of these relationships can be hurtful, with love flowing from one aspect often not enough to compensate for a hole elsewhere. Fulfilled emotional-hunger helps society, because an emotionally content person feels worthy and secure, has a healthy sense of self, and helps others feel emotionally fulfilled.

Not uncommonly I hear from people, "Everything is good in my life. My spouse loves me; I don't have any major health issues. I feel financially secure. But I'm not happy. Something is missing from life." That something is creativity. Zoo animals, if they aren't challenged with new toys and fun activities, get bored and die sooner. Our mind also likes challenges that stretch our imagination and focus. Absent such challenges, we become dull because of unfulfilled creativity-hunger.

With the above four hungers fulfilled, you might think that life would become hunky-dory. If that were the case, the rich and famous people who do interesting things would never feel miserable to the point of contemplating suicide or actually taking their lives. What they are missing is a deeper meaning. We are a meaning-seeking species. We crave to serve a meaning larger than ourselves. Deprived of such meaning, either because the meaning doesn't exist or we can't find it, we get melancholic. People find deeper meaning through serving fellow beings in a selfless manner (through work or otherwise), holding to faith, deepening understanding of the world, or following other means. A fulfilled meaning-hunger completes one's life.

In general, the more you feed your advanced hungers—those of love, creativity, and meaning—the less you need to satisfy the ego-hunger. Given the nature of my mind, I know I will always be hungry. Whenever I can, I should quench my creativity-hunger, which serves a higher meaning. I hope that'll provide me relative freedom from needing to overdose on food or ego. It will also help me see the love already flowing toward me. I wish the same for you.

May you feed your true hunger each day—the hunger of love, creativity, and meaning—to serve a purpose larger than yourself.

Take care.

Amit

* Suggested practice: Today, I will eat my meals while engaging all my senses.

(For additional practices, visit Stressfree.org/Immerse/)

Week 44

During this week you'll develop flexible preferences and strong principles and cultivate the courage to speak, listen, accept, and live by the truth.

87. Preferences

Be flexible about your preferences and strong in your principles.

Dear friend,

Flexibility helps you cultivate the quality of bending without breaking. The willow tree is a great model of optimal flexibility and strength. The tree has flexible branches that twist and turn in a storm but do not easily break. The tree also has robust roots that keep it strong and standing against sixty-mile-per-hour gales. The key to physical and psycho-spiritual resilience is to be optimally flexible and strong.

The resilient mind is flexible about preferences and strong in principles. I struggle with maintaining that disposition.

As I have grown older, I have become rigid about my preferences. Which side of the bed I sleep on, what time I eat, which route I take to work, which movies I watch, what I use as the opening screen on my computer, which flavor of toothpaste I use—all these are my preferences. If I nurture strong preferences and these conflict with someone else's, if neither will budge, that's a recipe for an argument or a clash. I don't like clashes.

I should be flexible about my preferences. I should balance my preferences with those of others. I should be careful about my preferences becoming a source of discomfort for others.

While a million preferences define my days, a few core principles are enough to run my entire life. Being grateful for the little and large (gratitude), being kind to one and all (compassion), working hard and taking failure and success in stride (acceptance), pursuing a meaning larger than myself (higher meaning), and having a low threshold before I forgive (forgiveness)—these are my five core principles.

In the end it boils down to the single universal principle—being kind. With commitment to kindness, I should free others from my preferences and become flexible, predictable, and easy going. That'll be a nice gift I can give to people whose lives I touch.

May you and the people around you be strong in principles and flexible in preferences.

Take care.

Amit

* Suggested practice: Today, I will remember a loved one's preference and try to fulfill it.
(For additional practices, visit Stressfree.org/Immerse/)

88. Truth

The unpleasant truth is infinitely more precious than pleasant farce.

Dear friend,

We live in an epidemic of lying. Research shows that about 60 percent of adults lie at least once in a ten-minute conversation. About 40 percent lie on their resumes, and 90 percent lie on their online dating profiles.

Lies come in various types. Some of the well-known types include cover-up, exaggeration, fabrication, fraud, omission, half-truth, and perjury. Lies conveyed to exaggerate one's credentials or get attention often reflect narcissistic disposition. Despite the bad press lies get, however, most lies are benign, particularly the ones spoken to avoid conflicts or prevent someone from getting physically or emotionally hurt. A lie spoken to avoid major discord and maintain law and order is often called a "noble lie."

Truth should always be the desired option. Truth, however, can taste bitter. When someone tells me, "Do you really want to hear the truth?" or "Let me tell you the truth," I often cringe. I cringe because here comes the deluge of bad news or negative feedback. I don't look at hearing the undesirable as, "Aha! Here is the opportunity to learn and grow."

Speaking the truth makes you vulnerable. Truth tellers are often seen as adversaries or tough nuts. My mind would rather hear the pleasant. Pleasantness is sweet to the ears. But sweetness isn't always healthy.

If I wish to hear the truth, I shouldn't trash the truth teller. I shouldn't tell others what I want to hear. I should open my arms to the truth and actively seek it. I should also integrate the truth into my life.

Choosing not to hear the truth isn't just a matter of preference. Ignorance can hurt a lot of people, particularly if you are in a position of power. Ignorance is also a poor escape from accountability. (Intentionally choosing not to learn about details that matter has a legal name—"willful blindness.") Many corporate leaders who drove their companies into the ground tried to use ignorance as their shield. But this was a cracked shield. They were rightly convicted of corporate fraud.

If I wish to grow, I need at least a few people who can tell me the facts as they are. I will only have such people around me if I am humble in receiving the reality as is. I should appreciate and adore the truth tellers, actively seek the truth, and correct my mistaken beliefs and actions. That is my only hope to be of greater value to the world.

May you have the courage to speak, listen to, and accept the truth; may you be surrounded by people who seek to listen to and speak the truth.

Take care.

Amit

*   Suggested practice: Today, I will truly value those who inform me about my mistakes.

(For additional practices, visit Stressfree.org/Immerse/)

Week 45

*D*uring this week you'll embrace your pain, feeling grateful that it came to you and not your children, and you'll find creative ways to connect your daily life with a deeper value.

89. Gratitude for Pain

When in pain, try to find gratitude that the pain came to you and not your children.

Dear friend,

I saw Chris, a sixty-five-year-old auto mechanic from rural Washington, as a walk-in patient on a Friday afternoon. He complained of water blisters at the bottom of his right foot. They had started a few weeks before. He also had long-standing diabetes. Chris said, "They don't hurt or nothin'; my wife just doesn't like the smell." The moment he removed his shoes, it was clear what we were dealing with. Chris had a serious foot infection. When I touched his feet, he had no pain. In fact, he could hardly feel my fingers. Chris needed aggressive antibiotic treatment, and during surgery a small metal fragment was found in his "water blister." He never felt it. He ended up losing his foot.

Every millimeter of our skin has touch, pain, and temperature receptors, ready to alarm us of potential danger. Some areas are more sensitive than others. When I step on a sharp nail, even before I can consciously feel the pain, my spinal reflex removes my foot. My system is always on guard for physical (and emotional) pain.

I need my pain. By sounding its alarm, the pain nudges me to act to protect my being from physical or psychological injury. Yet pain is distinctly unpleasant. I don't like to be in pain, particularly when I struggle to find meaning in it.

I can often find (or sometimes imagine) meaning in my pain, particularly when it isn't excruciating, doesn't become my fellow traveler for long, and does alert me about a real issue. But I struggle with finding meaning in the pain that hurts little children. They are guileless and innocent. Why should nature allow them to be in pain?

Further, like in all humans, my brain can't tell the difference between personal pain and the pain of someone I care about. As a result, seeing innocents in pain hurts me even more than my own pain.

I would love to always be pain-free. I know that isn't likely to happen. I wish most of my days are free of excruciating pain. I also hope my pain has meaning that justifies it. If I ever came to know that my pain prevented someone innocent from getting hurt, I would feel truly privileged. For now I find great relief in thinking that my pain came to me and not my children (or any other child). I pray I accept my every pain with this thought. I also pray that innocents never be in pain.

May the hurts you endure today not have the power to dismantle your commitment to gratitude and compassion.

Take care.

Amit

* Suggested practice: Today, I will send silent good wishes to everyone who might be hurting so their pain is lesser.
  (For additional practices, visit Stressfree.org/Immerse/)

90. Bless the Sneeze

Sprinkle deeper values in routine daily activities.

Dear friend,

The sneeze is a useful reflex to rid your nose of irritants. Coordinated by a sneezing center in the lower part of the brain (also called the brainstem), sneezing involves elevation of the tongue and lowering of the palate, thus causing partial closure of the mouth, along with rapid expulsion of air from the nose and the mouth. The expelled air can reach speeds of thirty to forty miles per hour (or more).

Unlike coughs, sneezes have a lot of associated myths. In India, sneezing is considered inauspicious if it occurs when one is starting a new venture or when someone is leaving the house. I also grew up learning that you sneeze when you are in someone's thoughts—the louder the sneeze, the more intense the remembrance. In ancient Greece, a sneeze was considered a prophetic sign from the Gods, of something good materializing.

Another myth associated with sneezing prompts us to say, "Bless you." This practice originated from the belief that during a sneeze one is vulnerable to evil spirits entering, or that blessing the person might prevent him or her from developing the flu, the plague, or sudden death. No matter the beliefs, I like the idea of connecting a routine occurrence with a nice thought or saying.

So, like most of you, I bless when people sneeze. I was thinking the other day, "Why don't I bless when people yawn or cough?" Perhaps I have picked a social norm and haven't creatively expanded it. If I could bless people on yawns and coughs, I might double my *bless yous* every day and start seeing others' yawns as motivators to send good wishes rather than signals that I am boring.

Expanding further, I need to connect my daily life with thoughtful practices that remind me of our sacredness. When washing hands, I could see a blessing in flowing water. Anywhere I sit, I could imagine I am within a sacred abode.

I can choose to see people with the same grace. I can imagine a two-year-old behind a sixty-year-old face. One of the children in my neighborhood will grow up to be a police officer, a nurse, a plumber, an electrical engineer, or a mail carrier. They all serve an important purpose, and I should look at each child and remember his or her phenomenal potential. I can carry this thought to the inanimate—I can choose to be awed by the uniqueness of each orange, see a sage in a tree, a selfless gift of nature in an apple, and the purity in each drop of water.

Once I start the habit of looking deeper, I might start seeing a taxi as a source of livelihood for a family of four and a telemarketer as someone who has to endure countless slurs. Thinking deeper might also help change my language. How about feeding two birds with a single grain rather than killing two birds with a stone, or calling a deadline an opportunity line?

Commit to connecting an ordinary event in your life with something profound.

May the ordinary daily events of life remind you of the profound truths you came here to learn.

Take care.

Amit

* Suggested practice: Today, I will assume blessings flowing into my home with the water in the tap.
  (For additional practices, visit Stressfree.org/Immerse/)

Week 46

*D*uring this week you'll minimize unhealthy comparisons and feel thankful for the simple and the mundane.

91. The Comparison Trap

Avoid the comparison trap.

Dear friend,

I want to feel good about myself. But I do a poor job at it. Ideally I should be happy about the good within me and admire the good in others. I do just the opposite.

When I see good in others, instead of admiring it, I experience low self-esteem and envy; when I think I am good, instead of being grateful, I become haughty and inflated.

Even worse, I am highly skilled at zeroing in on the not so good in others. I judge others in domains where I am the strongest (and they are the weakest). I judge myself in domains where I am the weakest (and they are the strongest). Both these comparisons make me miserable and depressed. I am caught in the comparison trap.

I compare because I want to know where I stand. I compare because I lack confidence. I compare because my earliest haunting memories are of being compared to a distant cousin who always scored 100 percent in math, never lost a pencil, never drank soda, and started flossing at the age of nine.

Comparison isn't inherently bad. Comparison helps you weigh options, separate wrong from right, and pick from among a number of choices. Comparison that inspires and admires can be a powerful force. My comparisons, however, are biased to see the imperfections.

The reality is that most people are strong in different ways. Society values particular strengths based on its present needs. If someone isn't highly valued today, it may be because his or her domains of strength are not aligned with the present societal needs. That doesn't change his or her intrinsic value.

I should recognize my weaknesses and soften my negative judgments about others. I should value others' intrinsic values, such as kindness, caring, sense of humor, presence, and creativity, instead of comparing myself with their success, looks, or net worth. When I do compare, I should take pride in others' strengths and my own. I should actively seek what is right and excellent. No athlete has ever won gold medals in both the hundred-meter sprint and wrestling at the same event. I should default to admiring and being inspired.

As for my near-perfect cousin who contributed to my childhood misery—I have come to know that someone was inflating his accomplishments. However, if I had known this fact at that time, I wouldn't have pushed harder to match up with him, and I would be selling tomatoes at a street corner today. I am grateful to him, and I should remember to be grateful (instead of envious) to everyone whose excellence inspires me today.

May you be accepted and admired for who you are; may you accept and admire others for who they are.

Take care.

Amit

* Suggested practice: Today, I will be truly happy in others' happiness. (For additional practices, visit Stressfree.org/Immerse/)

92. Easy

Appreciate what seems easy, since it often reflects insights obtained by years of toiling.

Dear friend,

I like it easy. Easy things don't strain my mind's muscles. But I easily discount them. As a result, I often take easiness for granted. It risks losing value, meaning, and the joy it might provide me.

Easiness is of two types. One is ease that serves my weakness, particularly my penchant for short-term gratification. The second comes when something that once was difficult now has become easy, as I have gained experience.

Calorie consumption, a sedentary lifestyle, challenge avoidance, uncontrolled frustration, unkind words, and passive recreations are all easy. Of late, acquiring information and operating powerful gadgets have also become easy. In general, easiness that serves my short-term gratification isn't healthy for the long term.

The other type of easiness is well earned, often after years of intense practice. Examples include cooking, creative work, driving, and meditation (if it ever becomes easy!). Such easiness is welcome because it reflects your diligence and talent and not the innate nature of the activity, which started off being difficult.

Research shows that after repeated practice, activities, such as swimming or driving, do not require as much conscious attention. The subcortical networks of the brain (which don't need conscious engagement) come to coordinate the same activity. That's the reason that, while you drive, you can control your car, talk with passengers, receive a phone call, listen to music, sip coffee, monitor the traffic, check directions, and speed while looking out for a police car. Think about doing any of this when you were a teenager and had just started driving. You would have been annoyed with the least distraction.

Technology is constantly making life easier for us. This is good and bad. Sending flowers by the click of a button or ordering furniture on the Internet saves time. But it takes away the joy of visiting the local furniture store, getting to know a friendly salesperson, chasing kids in the open space, letting your weight drop on plush mattresses you couldn't afford, and enjoying the very sweet complimentary hot chocolate that you would have never purchased yourself.

Ease also leaves our attention free to roam into the mind's wanderings. When all I have to do to fix my dinner is open the package and heat it up, I don't need to think, smell, feel, or be creative during cooking. I could accomplish the entire task with very little attention. (You won't believe me, but research shows that the time it takes to cook a fresh meal is about the same as the time required to heat up and serve a prepackaged meal.)

We don't need to convert easy into difficult. Instead, we should harness the time and energy we save from not having to hand wash the clothes or manually do the dishes to spend quality time with loved ones, immerse in creative activities, and pursue emotional and spiritual growth. That, I believe, is our species' destiny.

May you find time each day to invest in quality connections, immerse in creative activities, and pursue emotional and spiritual growth.

Take care.

Amit

* Suggested practice: Today, I will be grateful for electricity in my house.
(For additional practices, visit Stressfree.org/Immerse/)

Week 47

During this week you'll develop a healthier way to overcome your hurts, and you'll soften the instinct of perfectionism.

93. Healing Old Hurts

Revisit old wounds to heal them, not open them afresh.

Dear friend,

In the soil rich with fear, selfishness, greed, and ignorance, the seeds of unkind words and actions sprout. Such seeds, when they get lodged in a vulnerable mind, give birth to saplings of hurt. These saplings are initially weak. Your ability to reframe the situation—to focus on what went right within what went wrong, find meaning, and accept the situation for what it was—can prevent the saplings of hurt from taking root. I wish I were that wise.

Instead of launching a fresh, mature perspective, my mind feeds the sapling. In thinking of how the hurts could have been prevented, I focus less on what I learned from them and more on whom to blame. I lament the event, get angry, and think of ways to exact revenge. Ruminating on past hurts, I make my life miserable. I could do better than that.

I can learn from the ethics of good reporters and historians. A good reporter communicates all aspects of the truth, fairly and in an engaging fashion. Historians are reporters of the past. A good historian helps us understand the past, without needing to commend or condemn it. Good reporters and historians try their best not to be biased. I should look at my past with their eyes.

When I study human history, I get a recurring feeling of humility. I learn that even the best intentions and efforts fail, and that chance is tremendously powerful. Every person acts under unique constraints. Every action has unintentional and unpredictable consequences. Maybe the person who hurt me acted in innocent ignorance rather than the vicious intention that I assumed.

I should look at my past as historians look at human history. I should zoom out of my experience and try to see it in totality. If I can do that, I will see not only the hurtful words and actions but also their origins in underlying suffering, self-defense, and ignorance. I will truly and deeply find gratitude for the right within the wrong, develop compassion toward people hurt by the wrong, and have a lower threshold for acceptance. With this mind-set I might find greater meaning in the experience and give forgiveness a chance.

As a result, I will stop watering the hurts, so they will stop at the sapling stage and not become large trees with complex root systems and countless additional seeds that spawn fresh saplings.

History is humility packaged as a true story. Become a true historian of your past, with an intention to understand and heal. This perspective will help you cherish the happy moments, learn from adversity, and be grateful for both.

May you cherish the happy moments, learn from adversity, and be grateful for both.

Take care.

Amit

*   Suggested practice: Today, I will feel grateful for a million different hurts that could have happened but didn't.
(For additional practices, visit Stressfree.org/Immerse/)

94. Perfectionists

Can the grip of perfectionism be softened?

Dear friend,

Our three-year-old likes to put everything on the carpet—books, cookies, straws, toys, bowls, phones, cereal boxes, tablecloths, paper napkins—everything. Keeping up with her is enough to meet the American Heart Association's daily recommendations for physical activity. It also tests our patience.

One week, she became very sick—not the usual cough and cold, but a raging bacterial infection. Those few days our home was clutter-free and clean—ghostly clean. We didn't like it.

She recovered and bounced back faster than we could blink. The experience changed us. We now look at clutter in a much more favorable way. Most days we smile when we step on sticky Cheerios in a carpet fold. Spoons, pencils, and keys discovered behind the sofa have become moments to celebrate.

We had to go through an adversity to loosen our perfectionist grip. We should learn from this experience and be more proactive. We should still strive to do right; however, we need to broaden our definition of right. Our desire and effort toward perfection should enrich our lives, not suffocate us.

We have now devised a simple solution. We have three categories in which we place our priorities—perfect, preferred perfect, and flexible. We strive for perfection in values. Lying, cheating, envying, bad-mouthing—we want perfection in eliminating these from our lives. Kindness, compassion, thankfulness, patience, faithfulness to a partner—we want perfection in living these values.

A step below are aspects that are important yet not as critical—remembering memorable occasions, paying utility bills on time, reaching places on time, exercising, eating healthy—these and many more are preferred-perfect aspects of life. We never wish to make anyone wait or delay paying any bills, but we have received our share of utility-disconnection notices that we have managed to evade just in time. Recently, when our elder daughter received her third tardy ticket of the month at school, she came home and said with excitement, "Look at this; it is pink." We knew right then that we wouldn't achieve perfection in reaching the school on time anytime soon.

The third category contains preferences that may be considered trivial or a bit more important, depending on your lifestyle and idiosyncrasies. The color of the tablecloth, the brand of paper napkins, the precise layout of furniture at home, the type of melon—a million little details we can choose to be flexible about. Flexibility doesn't mean apathy; it means the ability to appreciate all the different colors of the rainbow and not limit yourself to a single one.

With this wise choosing and inner flexibility, you'll pick the right priorities, not annoy others by your rigidity. You'll enjoy the multiple flavors of life, and if a mistake happens, you will not consider it a sign of personal inadequacy but instead see it as a prompt to work harder. This will allow you to save energy to pursue your life's higher meaning.

Choosing not to improve can be a great improvement.

May you become a little more perfect by letting go of the striving for perfection.

Take care.

Amit

* Suggested practice: Today, I will try not to improve anyone in my family.
(For additional practices, visit Stressfree.org/Immerse/)

Week 48

*D*uring this week you'll soften your mind's tendency to constantly seek others' approval, and you'll see others as they wish to be seen—with kindness.

95. *Keep It Simple*

My life will be much simpler once I accept that I don't need everyone to approve all aspects of me.

Dear friend,

Shall I plunk down an extra $64 and upgrade from economy to economy comfort? That croissant looks delicious, but I am really not that hungry. Should I be friendly and initiate a conversation with the person sitting next to me or just stay quiet? Where should I keep my bag—in the overhead compartment or beneath the seat in front of me? Soda, apple juice, coffee, or just plain water—what do I really want? In a single flight, my brain faces dozens of conflicting decisions.

The brain is by design a conflicted organ. Our central limbic circuitry loves doughnuts and fears spiders—seeking short-term gratification and running away from perceived fears. Our higher cortical brain thinks of the long term, feels compassion, provides inhibitory control, and delays short-term gratification. The two work together in each experience, giving you different points of view. They also seed tremendous conflicts. Your kidneys, for example, have no conflicts about what to do right now, but your brain does, by its intrinsic design.

The conflicted design of the brain also affects the values I live by. I struggle between selfishness and selflessness, revenge and forgiveness, greed and contentment, fear and fearlessness. I am not consistent. Others are also inconsistent (because we all have conflicted brains)—in their preferences, motives, constraints, and fears—and that inconsistency guides their vision. No wonder I exist in as many versions as there are people seeing me.

Yet, I want to be approved, liked, appreciated, and loved by everyone who knows me.

That's a recipe for disappointment. Every eye views a different me based on what it is seeing and what it saw earlier. Eyes don't choose to be biased; that's how they are designed.

While I strive to gain approval of as many as possible, I should recognize that I will invariably fail in this effort. With my countless imperfections and the infinite ways by which others look at me, there is a good chance that several people will be looking at aspects of me that need improvement. Several of these aspects I don't even presently know. So I should see disapproval as an opportunity to grow. Those are the only times I will get to know the parts of me that need editing.

Why should I do this? Because it isn't about me. My physical being is finite and, in the big picture, almost completely irrelevant. I am a little brick in this vast castle of life, a brick that won't stand the test of time. I should simply serve my short-term purpose as I see it, take accolades and rejections with the same enthusiasm, and find in each of them opportunities to grow so I can better serve. That'll keep it simple.

May you not be inflated by accolades or deflated by rejections; may you receive more accolades than rejections.

Take care.

Amit

*   Suggested practice: Today, I will serve planet earth as my primary employer and my own conscience as my primary judge.
     (For additional practices, visit Stressfree.org/Immerse/)

96. True Seeing

See others as they wish to be seen.

Dear friend,

I hardly see others these days, let alone see their true self. This is partly because of my weak attention. Research shows that presently an average person can maintain sustained attention for only about eight seconds (compared to nine seconds for the goldfish). Our ability to alternate attention (as in multitasking) has replaced our sustained attention.

Weakened attention, by default, becomes superficial and wandering. A brain with weakened attention usually becomes busy in its own monologue. It has limited dispensable attention and patience to truly notice others. As a result it sees others not as they are but as it has already decided it will see them. That decision depends on the brain's current preferences.

My preferences depend on who I think I am. That's important because I am likely to become a near-identical twin of whoever I think I am. If I think I am a bundle of desires, I will look at others as objects to fulfill my desires. If I think I am a blob of kindness, I will look at others with intentional kindness.

My untrained automatic version marinates in wants. Every waking moment, my sensory receptors crave stimulation, carrying to my mind a message of pleasure and gratification. That's the animal within me, my limited self.

But I have within me a different, more intentional version. It still has wants, but mostly healthy and disciplined wants. Its conscious moments are crowded by the desire to be kind. Its wants support kindness. Guided by these wants, I see others within their circles of love. I see them as they wish to be seen. I see the good in them. I then start living in a different, kinder world.

I hope we all will live in a kinder inner world, so we can create a kinder outer world. We can, if we look at ourselves not as a bundle of desires but as a being of kindness.

May you treat yourself with kindness; may you help others treat themselves with kindness.

Take care.

Amit

* Suggested practice: Today, I will see the good in everybody. (For additional practices, visit Stressfree.org/Immerse/)

Week 49

*D*uring this week you'll carry no unhealthy wants, and you'll develop greater openness to learning, recognizing the limitations of your knowledge.

97. Admiring Beauty

Find freedom from unhealthy desires.

Dear friend,

Beauty is the perception of something as pleasing, particularly to the eyes. Things, experiences, and places considered beautiful are often evolutionarily associated with enhanced survival. Different cultures and generations have unique concepts of beauty. A very long neck, scars on the belly, stretched lips, or blue tattoos on the lips—all are hallmarks of beauty in different parts of the world. Beauty is truly in the eyes of the beholder.

Beautiful objects and people fall into two types—ones that create no desire in us and others that we crave to acquire. A full moon is one of the most gorgeous spectacles I have ever seen. The stars are equally dazzling, as are the flowers in the garden, and the rising sun. Their beauty creates no desire within me that I need to resist, because I am happy to see them as they are—with no intention of owning them. That isn't the case with many other objects or people I find gorgeous.

Seeing beautiful decorations, paintings, and people stirs the lake of the mind by creating desires. Such desires seed conflicts. The mind wants to own beautiful objects, expensive gadgets, and famous works of art. But I can't have them all. Yet my wants don't listen to rational arguments. These unquenched wants create a sense of angst or lack of fulfillment within me.

Researchers find that seeing beauty activates specific areas of the brain, particularly the medial orbitofrontal cortex. Seeing beauty also activates areas of the brain that coordinate hand movement—we literally reach out to get beautiful objects. We are thus biologically designed to seek beauty. I don't think I can shed this impulse. I can, however, modify it, in two ways.

First, I should look at inner beauty and not just outer loveliness. I should admire the purity of the mind, the innocence of the intentions, and the kindness of the soul. I should look at people as sacred beings, not just physical bodies.

Second, when I look at the physical aspects of people and objects of beauty, I should look at them as I look at the moon—with admiration and no craving. My wants should be in my control. Unchecked wants are a perfect source of distraction, away from virtue and toward a life full of greed, selfishness, and envy. I will be very sorry at the end of such a life, if I live just for selfish acquisition, with no other meaning to my existence. I should wake up today and align my seeking, not just with sensory pleasures, but with altruistic meaning. Tomorrow might be too late.

May you have the ability to admire beauty without carrying any unhealthy wants.

Take care.

Amit

* Suggested practice: Today, I will not fantasize about anything or anyone that doesn't belong to me. I will replace those fantasies with gratitude for what I have and those who belong to me.
(For additional practices, visit Stressfree.org/Immerse/)

98. Facts Are Opinions

Wisdom lies in asking deeper questions and, through search for the answers, becoming a better human being.

Dear friend,

Myths are widely held beliefs often related to the supernatural. Many myths are totally imaginary, while others are created to explain perceivable sensory experiences. Myths serve several very important roles. They connect us, provide shared beliefs, enrich our lives, and give us a reason to cooperate. Scientists believe that collective myths provided the glue that connected millions of people together so they could live in relative peace in big cities. Myths have thus played, and will continue to play, a critical role in the creation of just and peaceful societies.

Some myths are deeply comforting, dispelling our fears—such as the myths of fairy godmothers, angels, and friendly genies. Other myths increase our fears—such as the idea of the great flood that will drown the whole world, epic wars, dragons, vampires, and the apocalypse. Myths can be extraordinarily cute—my personal favorites are the myths of Santa Claus and the tooth fairy.

Santa Claus and the tooth fairy were real for our six-year-old, until she realized they were us, her parents. When she totally believed in Santa Claus and the tooth fairy, no evidence would convince her otherwise. Her happiness was invested in their being real. Evidence to the contrary would have challenged her sense of self.

Similar to our six-year-old, I have no doubt I carry countless beliefs I consider facts that are in reality just myths. Some are helpful and others less so. I won't become aware of the truth until I acknowledge my ignorance.

When we are locked in the certainty of myths, because they either dispel fears or create collective fears (which is one way to control others), the truth evades us. The first step to knowledge is to admit I don't know. The wisest among us are the ones most convinced of how little they know. Knowledge to them is like a river. It keeps flowing. Facts start as opinions, become facts, and then again become opinions. With enough repetition, wise people see facts as placeholders with different levels of certainty, which never reach 100 percent. That realization makes them flexible—open and flexible.

My facts don't have to be your facts. Maybe you are already a step ahead. I should shed my arrogance. Instead, I should open my gates of humility so I can learn—through opinions and facts—a thing or two about the learner. With humility I should ask deeper questions, such as, how was this world created? Or even more importantly, why was this world created?

The search for the answers will take you to the deepest place within you, deeper than where science and philosophy can go. While the ultimate *why* may be unanswerable, perhaps the magic may not be in finding that answer at all. The magic may be in searching for the answer, and through that search, becoming a humble, kind, gentle, and virtuous human being who embraces universal compassion.

May you ask deeper questions and search for deeper answers, and through that search, become a humble, kind, gentle, and virtuous human being.

Take care.

Amit

* Suggested practice: Today, I will respect others' opinions, which might be different from mine.
(For additional practices, visit Stressfree.org/Immerse/)

Week 50

During this week you'll pick the right battle—instead of emptying the mind, you'll choose to fill it with gratitude and compassion, and you'll clear the mind of its dirt—the negative thoughts.

99. The Right Battle

Try not emptying the mind; instead, fill it with kinder, happier, fewer thoughts.

Dear friend,

My eyes are designed to see; I can't stop them from seeing. My ears are designed to hear; I can't stop them from hearing. The same is true for my other senses and every other part of my body. My lungs breathe about twenty thousand breaths a day, and my heart beats about one hundred thousand beats a day. I can't (and shouldn't) tell my lungs to stop inflating and deflating or my heart to stop beating. Similarly, I can't tell my mind to stop thinking.

For the rest of my life, during each of my awake moments, I will experience two worlds—the outer world of objects and the inner world of thoughts. Just as I can't freeze the outer world, I can't silence my inner world. That isn't a battle I should be fighting.

Instead, I should redirect my flow of thoughts. I should think thoughts that are lush with meaning, that breathe gratitude and compassion and bring peace to others and myself. I should take charge of my thinking, which means thinking more intentional thoughts. But I haven't exercised that choice yet. My mind is thus busy in its default state, thinking instinctive thoughts—about people, daily chores, trivial details, selfish interests. I find this state dissatisfying.

I should choose my thoughts and not let thinking happen to me. This will give a nice haircut to my thoughts, so that the unnecessary or the toxic ones will find no reason to stay, while the ones present will become more positive, more productive, and deeper. It will make my mind more beautiful.

A more thoughtful mind has fewer thoughts. Such a mind will help you be a person free of unhealthy wants and fears.

Telling the mind not to think is like telling the heart not to beat. Pick the right battle in your life—don't silence your mind; instead, cultivate a mind that thinks kinder, happier, and fewer thoughts.

May you think thoughts you are proud to own.

Take care.

Amit

* Suggested practice: Today, I will send silent compassion to every child in pain.
(For additional practices, visit Stressfree.org/Immerse/)

100. Reframing My Hurts

Let your moments of pain remind you to practice deeper gratitude, compassion, acceptance, meaning, and forgiveness.

Dear friend,

Acute back pain, particularly the kind where one wrong twist can send you into severe pain, changes every aspect of life, at least for a few days. Sitting, lying, walking, eating, sleeping—during every single activity, you protect yourself from the pain.

Emotional pains are the same. An emotional pain, strong enough to draw your attention for the better part of the day, becomes the defining thought for the day. Further, while most acute backaches are short-term visitors, emotional pains can find a home in our brains for a lifetime because of our phenomenal memory of negative events and ability to imagine and catastrophize.

It doesn't have to be this way. A multitude of salves, made of time-less values, can heal the emotional pain. The balm of gratitude helps you remember that the hurt could have been much worse. My shoul-der pain could have been not just the muscle sprain but metastatic cancer. I should be grateful that it isn't metastatic cancer and focus on that reality rather than the pain itself.

The emollient of compassion helps me remember millions who have pain worse than mine, no one to empathize, no rest from work despite the pain, and suboptimal treatments. When I focus on compassion for them, I help palliate my own pain.

I should also recognize that of the 360 joints and 650 muscles, one or two will at times get sore in this almost fifty-year-old frame. I can either fight this reality or just accept it. With acceptance a light shines, which lets me find meaning in my pain. Maybe my pain is signaling that I should become more disciplined about keeping myself fit; maybe it is preventing something worse that I don't even know about. With gratitude, compassion, acceptance, and meaning, I rewrite the scripts. Eventually I will have to arrive at a place where I erase the hurts—by forgiveness.

Forgiveness is the curative surgery that completely removes the hurts from life. Forgiveness clears the mind of negativity so love can find a place in it. The mind can't purify itself of hurtful emotions until it learns to forgive. Until I and others around me are perfect, I will keep getting hurt. I should accept this reality. Educated and empowered by this acceptance, I should learn to forgive, if I wish to remain light, free, and fully available to experience the magic of life.

May your hurts spur you to deepen your anchor in timeless values; may a deeper anchor in timeless values decrease your hurts.

Take care.

Amit

* Suggested practice: Today, I will use higher meaning to rethink my life's difficulties.

(For additional practices, visit Stressfree.org/Immerse/)

Week 51

$\mathcal{D}$uring this week you'll live with the hope that your good intentions will touch others, and you'll develop a healthier attitude toward anger.

101. My Hope

$\mathcal{D}$o everything you can to protect yourself from the hurtful action without letting go of compassion for the ignorance that prompted the hurtful action.

Dear friend,

I was sitting on a low stool looking to the right. Suddenly someone pushed me from the left, hurtling me to the ground. I fell on the floor, doubling up with pain. That someone was my playful nine-year-old. As I recovered, I noticed my daughter was crying. She was emotionally hurt because she had caused me pain. That's our natural instinct. When we hurt someone, physically or emotionally, intentionally or unintentionally, we hurt ourselves.

Research shows that your brain senses other people's pain as its own. Specifically, your brain's pain-processing areas (particularly the insula) activate when you perceive other brains' pain areas activating. This is particularly true for people you care about and love.

I should recognize the wisdom in this science. The person who hurt me actually hurt him- or herself. There may be a time lag in this realization, but it will eventually catch up with the person. My default should not be to seek revenge, for revenge won't undo my previous hurt, nor will it teach me or that person anything new. Revenge will only seed future reasons for hurling hurts. I should instead be compassionate to that person.

I should focus on his or her benign intentions, if they were indeed benign. For intentional hurts, I should recognize their origin in ignorance and, while doing everything I can to protect myself, be compassionate for that ignorance.

With my kindness for others, I will more easily find kindness for myself. I will uncover gratitude and meaning and thus come to acceptance and forgiveness. All these will help inspire the perpetrator to be kind.

There are situations where I have to put up a fight. In most circumstances, I have found the best weapon is kindness.

May you need no other weapon than kindness to negotiate (and win) your daily battles.

Take care.

Amit

* Suggested practice: Today, I will keep the hope that by being kind, I am helping the world be kind.
  (For additional practices, visit Stressfree.org/Immerse/)

102. Healthy Anger

Harness your anger so it seeds transformation, not regrets.

Dear friend,

Just as baboons show their canines, kitties hiss, screech, and beat their tails, and frogs puff themselves up when angry, humans lower their eyebrows, thin their lips, flare their noses, and push up their chins—all designed to convey the message, "Watch out; I have great fighting power."

Anger can range from mild displeasure or frustration to fuming rage that can become explosive and violent. The higher the temperature, the greater the element of fear and panic mixed in the anger. Anger is a way to vent and feel a sense of control. Not uncommonly, in our effort to blow off steam, we misdirect our anger. We don't get angry with those we *should* be angry with. We get angry with those we *can* be angry with. The latter are often the weak and the vulnerable.

Not all anger is bad, however. Many scientists theorize that anger was designed to increase social bargaining power. Gentle anger thus can be a great negotiating tool. It is a call for change. A reason often sparks such anger, often preceded by a larger story. Similarly, anger against injustice, oppression, or severe wrongs is often justified. Justifiable, gentle anger (details below) prevents violence instead of causing it, by providing a warning before things get worse. Indeed, research shows that most anger (90 percent) does not result in violence.

There are situations, however, where anger is maladaptive. For instance, violent anger can lead to a brawl and much worse. Such anger constricts attention, thereby interfering with the open-minded and free thinking that is necessary to find creative solutions. It is also energy intensive; you can't sustain such anger for more than a few minutes before feeling depleted. In violent anger, we lose rationality and kindness and seed future embarrassment, particularly if we misdirect it. Further, violent anger seldom serves the reason that evokes it. Instead, it inflames a part of us while improving no one. It provokes counter anger. It isolates us from the world. That's a heavy price to pay.

A second form of maladaptive anger is the repressed anger that bottles up negative emotions. While it may not hurt immediately, it has long-term consequences, including an increased risk of heart attacks and even early death. It creates inner conflicts, distances you from your loved ones, and sometimes incites passive-aggressive behavior.

How best to work with situations that invite maladaptive anger? I suggest two healthier options.

1. Elevate your anger threshold: The simplest and best alternative is to elevate your anger threshold so you aren't easily riled by common life situations. The more grateful, compassionate, accepting, and forgiving you are, the higher your anger threshold will be. Completely bypassing anger, however, is not only superbly difficult but also undesirable.

2. Develop justifiable, gentle anger: Be rational in your anger, dial down your anger energy, and direct that energy toward solutions. Slow down, step back, think two steps forward, look at the whole context, and follow these five principles: right reason, right person, right place and time, right extent, and right intention.

   Get angry for the right reason, with the right person, at the right place and time, to the right extent, and with the right intention. The reason should be substantial; the person should be the intentional wrongdoer; the place should be private; the time should be one conducive to learning; the extent should be proportionate to the perceived misdeed; and the intention should be to communicate the truth and to inspire.

If you follow these rules, your anger will be more effective. Such anger will less likely seed future regrets or embarrassments. It will also help you reach a point where you don't bottle up internal anger. That might remove toxic arguments, conflicts, and fights from your life and fill the space so created with love, nurturing, and meaning. Won't that be nice?

May you seldom get angry; may your occasional anger seed transformation, not regrets.

Take care.

Amit

* Suggested practice: Today, I will be the gentlest I can be if I become angry.
(For additional practices, visit Stressfree.org/Immerse/)

Week 52

During this week you'll shed your idea of perfection in favor of humility, and you'll aspire to become instinctively compassionate.

103. A Bad Day

Shed your idea of perfection, because it depends on your imperfections.

Dear friend,

One of my core fears is that someday I will think that I have become nearly perfect. That will be a very bad day because such a belief will signal that I have become steeped in ignorance and ego, which is decidedly going backward. I try my best to stay away from that possibility.

Another core fear is that someday I will start to expect perfection from others. Expecting perfection from others is synonymous with expecting them to do exactly as I want them to do. That is oxymoron because my idea of others' perfection depends on my own imperfections.

Seeking perfection, for self or others, by itself isn't wrong, as long as you carefully pick what you want to be perfect about. You don't want your aircraft pilot to be casual about the particulars related to landing the plane, and you don't want the neurosurgeon to leave some of the procedural details to chance. Perfection in practicing kindness toward your partner is desirable. We all depend on someone's perfection every day to remain safe and alive. Hence, we shouldn't nurture a blanket criticism of perfection.

But if we invest all our meaning in a trivial detail, such as the crease of the pants, the precise configuration in which to load the dishwasher, or the knot in the tie, then we set ourselves up for anxiety and depression. With such a disposition, faced with even a small failure, we feel unworthy and unlovable. We begin to hold ourselves to unrealistic standards and globalize our mistakes.

I have a better alternative. I should free others from my preferences. I should recognize our collective imperfections; in fact, I should stop calling the oddities *imperfections.* Who gets to decide what they are? Perhaps they are our uniqueness or predispositions or adornments. The recognition of human ignorance created a seismic shift in scientific progress several hundred years ago, helping us break free from some of the dogmas that handcuffed us. Ignorance, an imperfection, when approached with humility and acceptance, transformed into science. Our imperfections thus can seed our transformation.

I believe that when I'm fully seeped in this wisdom, I'll find an easier path to acceptance. With acceptance, I will experience fewer hurts, decreasing instances in which I need to forgive. Once I arrive at such awareness, I will have become a little less imperfect.

May you never feel that you are perfect; may you never desire someone else to be perfect.

Take care.

Amit

* Suggested practice: Today, I will not hold others to my preferences. (For additional practices, visit Stressfree.org/Immerse/)

104. Instinctive Compassion

Let compassion become your habit so you do not need intentional effort to be compassionate.

Dear friend,

Joey, right after birth, climbs into his mother's pouch. Leatherback turtle babies need no instruction to walk toward the ocean after they emerge from the eggs. Human moms come preprogrammed with countless skills to care for their young. These complex behaviors, which are innate to us and have obvious survival value, are called our *instincts*.

We learn another set of complex behaviors. These entail exercise of a choice. Declining a bowl of ice cream or french fries, forgiving, performing random acts of kindness—these are learned behaviors that need *intentionality*. Intentionality is the hallmark of a more complex brain. Intentionality is unique to us humans. Intentionality needs deeper thought, often with an active focus on the long term.

Our strongest instincts focus on self-preservation and procreation. Behaviors guided by fear, greed, and selfishness, to preserve and expand what I consider me and mine, dominate my day. A world that works by this rule will remain depleted of altruistic intentions. When everyone is busy taking out energy, who's putting it back in?

Intentional compassion can offer moments of respite in such a world, but because intentionality is energy intensive, it may not be frequent enough to compensate for instinctive selfishness. That's the main problem with intentionality—it is effortful and energy intensive. In the tug-of-war between instincts and intentionality, most days instincts win, since instincts need the least amount of attention and energy.

We have to create a world where compassion is the first and most primal instinct. In such a world, I will focus on your pain and you on mine, with both of us wanting to heal each other's pain. Creation of such a world has to be the legacy of a species as brainy and creative as ours. Once a critical mass of us breathes compassion in and out, it will become the defining force for the world. I hope I am alive when that happens. I hope you are there too.

May the world become more compassionate because you live in it.

Take care.

Amit

*   Suggested practice: Today, I will send silent compassion to at least one person who I know is suffering.
(For additional practices, visit Stressfree.org/Immerse/)

Final Thought

Surrender

Replacing intellect with surrender is a good bargain.

Dear friend,

I can read, write, predict, remember, analyze, decide, create, imagine, and entertain. I am not a genius but am not entirely dumb. From the time I became conscious of my presence, I have been busy trying to prove to the world that I am intelligent and worthy of attention. I may have somewhat succeeded in that endeavor. But lately I am realizing how limited, almost phony, I am.

I read but do not understand, write words that often don't make sense, predict but to a very rough approximation, remember but soon forget, analyze but with great incompleteness, decide but without conviction, create but only the ordinary and the barely useful, and imagine but within three dimensions. I am terrible at entertaining.

Most of all, I can do nothing to take the pain away from someone half a world away. I have no idea how the world will be in a day, an hour, or the next moment. I am severely limited.

I give up. I give up my obsession with control. I give up my love of intellect. I give up the desire to be right. This giving up relieves me.

In that giving up, I find the freedom that I have been looking for—the freedom of surrender.

I surrender. I surrender to a higher intellect that created and can protect all the world's children. I can't. Who breathes air into our children's lungs when they (and we) sleep? I know not. I truly respect and love that power. I surrender to the intellect that created the dimensions. I don't know if that intellect is formed or formless, or where it resides. I won't name it, since I can't fathom it.

Perhaps that intellect is probability or providence or destiny or nature or consciousness or intentionality or emptiness or something else. Poets, philosophers, scientists, believers, citizens—we all have different names for what we consider larger than ourselves. Let's not quibble about the names. For this intellect unites us all. Its nature is wisdom and love—wisdom that teaches universal interconnectedness and love that teaches universal compassion. We sorely need wisdom and love to help our children thrive in a caring world that we collectively create. I am grateful to you for your contribution to the creation of such a world.

I am also grateful that I have the intellect to recognize my intellect's limitations. I am grateful I can think of surrender before I lose the ability to surrender.

May the power of surrender empower you for passionate action.

Take care.

Amit

*   Suggested practice: Today, I will live in a state of surrender. (For additional practices, visit Stressfree.org/Immerse/)

Acknowledgments

A book is a letter from an author to the readers. The words in a book often tell a story filled with facts, insights, humor, and love.

I am grateful to the countless scientists, reporters, philosophers, and authors who have helped me learn the facts I share in this book. I am particularly grateful to my colleague and friend, Professor Kristin Vickers-Douglas for her thoughtful insights on this book.

I am grateful to my colleagues at Mayo Clinic who have supported my work all these years. My special thanks to:

Mayo Complementary and Integrative Medicine Program colleagues—Drs. Brent A. Bauer, Anjali Bhagra, Sherry S. Chesak, Tony Y. Chon, Jon C. Tilburt; Debbie L. Fuehrer, Barbara (Barb) S. Thomley, Susanne M. Cutshall, Shelley M. Noehl, Kathryn C. Heroff and rest of the team—for providing support and inspiration.

Mayo Division of General Internal Medicine team—Drs. Paul S. Mueller, Christopher M. Wittich; Rachel L. Pringnitz, Pamela J. Bowman, Beth A. Borg—for being the solid quarterbacks to everything I do.

Mayo Department of Medicine team—Drs. Morie A. Gertz and colleagues—for inspiration and extraordinary support.

Mayo Medical School colleagues—Drs. Alexandra P. Wolanskyj, Lotte N. Dyrbye, Michele Y. Halyard, Robin Molella; Mary E. Sheeran, Sarah J. Hager, Shelby L. Strain, Marcia L. Andresen Reid, and other team members—for helping our medical students achieve their academic and life goals.

Mayo legal and brand team—Monica M. Sveen Ziebell and Amy L. Davis—for going above and beyond in helping me each step of the way.

Mayo leadership—Dr. John H. Noseworthy and Jeffrey W. Bolton—for tirelessly working to promote the inspiring vision that drives Mayo Clinic each day.

Every employee at Mayo Clinic, for working together to truly live the spirit of our mission: "The best interest of the patient is the only interest to be considered."

I am grateful to every person who has helped me smile, smiled at my sometimes not-so-funny jokes, and helped me keep a light heart so I could sprinkle some humor in this book.

I am grateful to Carla Paonessa and Judith Paul for their friendship and support.

I am grateful to all my friends; my parents, Sahib and Shashi; my in-laws, Vinod and Kusum; my brother, Kishore; my sisters, Sandhya and Rajni; my daughters, Gauri and Sia; and my wife, Richa, for showering me with love that I could bring to this book.

I am grateful to you all for helping build a kinder, happier, and more hopeful world for our planet's children. Thank you.

Amit

About Dr. Sood

*D*r. Amit Sood is married to his love-ly wife of 23 years, Dr. Richa Sood. They have two girls, Gauri age 11 and Sia age 5.

Dr. Sood holds the rank of professor of medicine in Mayo Clinic College of Medicine. He serves as chair of the Mind Body Medicine Initiative and provides stress management and resiliency consults to patients at Mayo Clinic.

Dr. Sood completed his residency in internal medicine at the Albert Einstein School of Medicine, an integrative medi-cine fellowship at the University of Arizona and earned a master's degree in clinical research from Mayo Clinic College of Medicine. He has received several National Institutes of Health grants and foundation awards to test and implement integrative and mind-body ap-proaches within medicine.

Dr. Sood has developed an innovative approach toward mind-body medicine by incorporating concepts from neuroscience, evolutionary biology, psychology, philosophy and spirituality. His resulting program, Stress Management and Resiliency Training (SMART©) helps patients learn skills to decrease stress and enhance resiliency by improving self-awareness (i.e. brain awareness), cultivating intentional attention (engagement) and developing values-based thinking (emotional resilience). Interventions adapted from the program reach approximately 50,000 patients and learners each year. The program has been tested in 20 completed and 6 ongoing clinical trials.

Dr. Sood's programs are offered to a wide variety of patients and learners including to improve resiliency; decrease stress and anxiety; enhance well-being and happiness; cancer symptom relief and prevention; and wellness solutions for caregivers, corporate executives, health care professionals, parents, and students. SMART© program is now part of the curriculum for Mayo Medical School, and is offered enterprise wide to enhance physician wellbeing and professionalism, and for enhancing resilience among nurses. The program is also being offered to middle and high school students to enhance their focus and wellbeing.

Dr. Sood has authored or co-authored over 70 peer-reviewed articles, and several editorials, book chapters, abstracts and letters. He has developed award-winning patient education DVDs on topics within integrative medicine ranging from paced breathing meditation and mindfulness to wellness solutions for obesity, insomnia and fibromyalgia. He is credited with developing several courses for incorporating concepts of integrative medicine within conventional medical curriculum and introduced the first Mayo Clinic iPhone app for meditation training. Dr. Sood is author of the books *The Mayo Clinic Guide to Stress-Free Living* and *The Mayo Clinic Handbook for Happiness.*

As an international expert in his field, Dr. Sood's work has been widely cited in the press including – *The Atlantic Monthly, USA Today, Wall Street Journal, New York Times, NPR, Reuters Health, Time Magazine (online), Good Housekeeping, Parenting, Real Simple, Shape, US News, Huffington Post, Mens Health Magazine, The Globe and Mail, CBS News, Fox News, and others.* He has interviewed with several prominent TV and radio shows, both nationally and internationally. He served as the February 2015 Health care pioneer for the Robert Wood Johnson Foundation.

He is highly sought after as a speaker, presenting more than 100 workshops each year. He recently delivered the TEDx talk – *Happy Brain: How to Overcome Our Neural Predispositions to Suffering.* He has mentored several hundred fellows, medical students, instructors, consultants, and residents. Dr. Sood has received several awards for his work, including the Mayo's 2010 Distinguished Service Award, Mayo's 2010 Innovator of the Year Award, Mayo's 2013 outstanding physician scientist award, and was chosen as one among the top 20 intelligent optimists "helping the world be a better place" by *Ode Magazine.*

About the SMART Program
(http://stressfree.org/programs/smart/)

SMART (Stress Management and Resiliency Training) is a structured approach to enhance engagement and emotional intelligence based on cutting-edge advances in neurosciences. Dr. Sood developed this program by integrating concepts from neurosciences, evolutionary biology, psychology, philosophy, behavioral economics, decision-making, and spirituality.

Research shows human attention instinctively focuses on threats and imperfections. Since a considerable amount of threat exists within the domains of the past and the future, attention inordinately gets engaged in the ruminative mind. Human interpretation (thinking process) is guided by prejudices, values and preferences. Invariant rigid biases that one is unwilling to renegotiate despite evidence to the contrary disengage the mind from the novelty of the present moment and increases reward (happiness) threshold. These biases prevent the individual from fully engaging with 'what is.'

In the SMART program, participants learn a structured approach to decrease stress and enhance resilience in two steps:

1. The Basics – As a first step, participants develop a pragmatic understanding of the brain processes underlying human attention. The training elaborates on the information about the brain's default mode of mind wandering where we spend half our day (or more), and our innate focus on threats and imperfections. The workshop explores reasons behind the mind's restlessness and irrationality, and the paradox of thought suppression causing recoil of the same thought.

2. The Skills – The program offers two core set of skills – Engagement (Intentional attention) and Emotional Resilience (Values-based thinking).

   • Engagement – Positive engagement entails authentic, undistracted and intentional attention. Participants learn three core skills that take a total of five minutes during the day to deepen their attention, enhance personal relationships, and bring a more authentic presence.

   • Emotional Resilience – Participants learn an approach to enhance gratitude focus, nurture greater compassion, creatively work with 'what is,' explore life's higher meaning, and strengthen forgiveness skills.

The program shares application of these skills to daily life, both personal and professional. The program has been scientifically proven in twenty clinical trials to decrease symptoms of stress and anxiety and increase well-being, resilience, self-regulation, mindfulness, happiness, and positive health behavior (http://stressfree.org/research/).

SMART workshops are taught both online and in person. Depending on the intensity and depth of teaching, the workshops durations include – 60 minutes, two hours, half a day, full day and two days. SMART is also commonly offered as a keynote in different conferences. A typical schedule for a 60-minute workshop is:

1. Introduction – 10 minutes
2. The Basics
    The Brain's two modes – 5 minutes
    Our negativity bias – 5 minutes
    SMART Model – 5 minutes
3. The Skills
    Engagement (Intentional Attention) – 20 minutes
    Emotional Resilience (Values-based thinking) – 10 minutes.
4. Take Home Message, Next Steps – 5 minutes

The SMART program is currently offered to over five thousand patients every year at Mayo Clinic and over fifty thousand participants every year globally. Some of the attractive features of the SMART program include:

- Science driven
- Relationship centric
- Values based
- Emphasis on simplicity and ease of learning
- Practical and relevant for 21st century
- Secular
- Entertaining
- Needs minimal time commitment
- Highly scalable
- High engagement
- Availability of train-the-trainer course (http://Stressfree.org/courses/).

48350396R00170

Made in the USA
San Bernardino, CA
23 April 2017

Made in the USA
Lexington, KY
23 December 2016